How To Master Your Mental Game in Sports

Jennifer Heistand

BALBOA.PRESS

A DIVISION OF HAY HOUSE

Balboa Press books may be ordered through booksellers or by contacting:

Balboa Press
A Division of Hay House
1663 Liberty Drive
Bloomington, IN 47403
www.balboapress.com
844-682-1282

Because of the dynamic nature of the Internet, any web addresses or links contained in this book may have changed since publication and may no longer be valid. The views expressed in this work are solely those of the author and do not necessarily reflect the views of the publisher, and the publisher hereby disclaims any responsibility for them.

The author of this book does not dispense medical advice or prescribe the use of any technique as a form of treatment for physical, emotional, or medical problems without the advice of a physician, either directly or indirectly. The intent of the author is only to offer information of a general nature to help you in your quest for emotional and spiritual well-being. In the event you use any of the information in this book for yourself, which is your constitutional right, the author and the publisher assume no responsibility for your actions.

Any people depicted in stock imagery provided by Getty Images are models, and such images are being used for illustrative purposes only. Certain stock imagery © Getty Images.

Print information available on the last page.

ISBN: 978-1-9822-6192-4 (sc)
ISBN: 978-1-9822-6191-7 (e)

Balboa Press rev. date: 12/15/2022

Contents

Dedication

I dedicate this book to my son, Bouldin, and all the athletes who will benefit from the information within. Without Bouldin's encouragement, it would never have seen the light of day.

There are so many athletes who do not have the resources available to hire a mental performance professional. Know that we sometimes overcome our greatest challenges and realize our dreams with no one to depend upon but ourselves.

I hope that once you have gained your own solid footing and have leveled up your game, you will pass this awareness to others. I have so much appreciation for each and every one of you. Thank you.

Introduction

Sports are Played with the Body, but Won with the Mind

Are you an athlete who has hit a wall getting to the next level? Or are you an athlete who has let your mental game get in the way of your performance? If so, this book is for you.

Every day you have a chance to be better than the day before. With the tools and knowledge I will share with you, each day will feel as if it is a fresh start in your career.

The name of my company is StillPoint Performance. I instruct athletes every day about what it means to be in the still point of their own mind. But I wanted to make sure other athletes had the same access to the information my clients have. When your mind is at the point of stillness, you are no longer trying to manage your thoughts or losing control of your emotions.

When inner silence has liberated you from the constant chatter that suffocates your conscious thoughts, you will find yourself playing your sport with ease and a "flow" (in the zone) that most athletes experience only rarely.

This book is designed so you can learn the inner workings of your mind and body in order to enhance your performance to the best of its ability.

Some mental performance books will only tell you *what* should be done to improve your mental game. Here, you will learn *why* emotions cause involuntary actions before I tell you *how* to *do* the things I'm asking of you.

You cannot correct a mistake until you have learned why it is taking place to begin with. This is why many athletes who have previously seen other mental performance coaches or read their books recognize that the improvements are not sustainable over a long period of time.

Once I explain the inner workings of your mind and body, you will begin to understand why certain thoughts or unwanted emotions keep rising to the surface. By forming new habits and employing the techniques I'll share, you will quickly be able to identify the source of the mental distraction and pull yourself instantly back into a coherent thought process again.

Within the chapters of this book, you will be given tools to assist you in your emotional management. You will not only improve your game, but the quality of your life as well.

In language that will speak directly to you as an athlete, I'll teach you to

- understand how emotional intelligence can affect you, both personally and professionally;
- use positive emotions to improve yourself as a person and as a player;
- prepare for and recover from stress and adversity;
- understand the various chemicals your body produces and how they affect both your habits and thought processes;
- reach your full potential by discovering what you love about your game and where your motivation comes from;

- train yourself mentally to achieve more consistent results;
- overcome ingrained preconceptions about yourself to develop genuine confidence;
- develop habits that will align with your goals;
- understand and hone the emotions required to become a clutch player; and
- use visualizations to put you in the place where you have the best chance to succeed.

You will learn that emotions such as anxiety, anger, or frustration not only affect your thought processes, they also have a direct link to your coordination and physical ability on the playing field. Anxiety, anger, and frustration cause the signals in the nervous system to become erratic and, as a result, will drive you into fight or flight mode.

To the surprise of most athletes, they are not doing a physical action incorrectly; it is a negative mental thought or emotion that is causing them to repeatedly come up short.

When I start working with my athletes and they begin to understand these facts, it comes as a great relief. And results begin to appear almost immediately.

This book does not single out one sport, only the athlete's mind, which is the true universal playing field. So, whether you are playing with a tennis ball, golf ball, football, or baseball, or if you are running around a track, you will be able to use this book to positively affect your mental game, on and off the field.

CHAPTER 1

What Having Emotional Intelligence Means

I know that I'm never as good or bad as any single performance. I've never believed my critics or my worshippers, and I've always been able to leave the game at the arena.

–Charles Barkley

Emotional intelligence is a term you are hear more and more often in books and on social media. The reason is simple: people—especially athletes—are starting to realize and admit that their emotional reactions are affecting both their personal lives and their athletic performances. As athletes develop their physical game with the guidance from their coaches, they are now being heavily encouraged to also master their mental game.

While we've reached the point where people now recognize having emotional intelligence is an advantage, a term that has *not* become a buzzword is "emotional regulation." One might believe that if they had emotional intelligence, they would automatically know what it means to have emotional self-regulation.

However, this is not the case. Only the most self-aware athletes or those who have had mental coaching are aware of how to use their emotions to their advantage. Possessing the knowledge to self-regulate allows the athlete to recognize when they have let a screwup or negative thought get into their head and to proactively change their emotional response in a direction that will bring them back into mental coherence.

The perfect example is the basketball player whose shots are simply not going in during a particular game. The frustration is clearly building. But instead of continuing to fire away from a distance, the astute player will change course and drive to the basket in the hopes of drawing a foul. Once at the free-throw line, just seeing a simple shot go through the hoop is often enough to steady the player's mind.

In order to learn how to use self-regulation, you must first understand what it means to have emotional intelligence. Fewer than 40 percent of people can actually identify their emotions as they are experiencing them.

StillPoint Insight #1

When you learn to control your moments,
your moments will not control you.

Everyone has emotions; we experience them 95 percent of our waking hours. The startling fact is that most individuals bounce from one emotion to the next without recognizing that these reactive emotions are having an impact on their daily lives.

Having emotional intelligence means understanding the significance of an emotion to you and becoming aware of how each emotion is affecting you and your game. It also means you're consciously aware when you are having a negative emotional response and you can identify the driving force behind the heightened emotion.

Most of the players affected by this are experiencing internal emotional interruptions. In a nutshell, this means a commentary is taking place inside their head, either berating themselves for a failed execution or overthinking a possible future outcome. Again, the majority of players react internally, while others take it a step further and reacting externally—which every opponent knows is their window of opportunity.

A pitcher watching a frustrated hitter snap his bat across his knee after striking out for the third time in the game confidently knows that the hitter has mentally checked out, unlikely to be a threat for the rest of the day.

This is a case where the athlete cannot control their emotions. They speed through their internal emotional response and crash into the external emotional response. There they will act out, displaying an emotional outburst for everyone to see.

For instance, last year I was at a tennis tournament watching two of my clients, when I heard loud obnoxious yelling coming from the court behind me. At first, I thought a young athlete was shouting at his opponent, but once I got drawn into the scene (like a moth to a flame), I soon realized he was on the court having a very humorous conversation with himself. In front of his parents, coach, and anyone within shouting distance, he was belittling himself in the third person. "Oh yeah, Billy, you really are sucking up the court now," he said to himself. "You see, Dad, this is why you've paid thousands of dollars, so Billy can stink up the court in front of his girlfriend." It went on from there. And yes, Billy did lose the match.

I have been a witness to this type of third-person talk display numerous times. Hell, I have even done it myself while playing tennis a few times. However, Billy's demonstration is the perfect example of an external emotional response.

External emotional responses not only affect the athlete; they also affect the athlete's teammates and their overall morale. In the recruitment of both college and professional players, it is becoming more common in sports to look at the emotional mindset of a player than ever before.

An extreme example of this playing out happened in 2019, in an early-season, Thursday Night Football tilt between the Pittsburgh Steelers and Cleveland Browns. With the Browns up twenty-one to seven with eight seconds left, the game was all but wrapped up. Cleveland defensive end Myles Garrett ripped the helmet off Steelers quarterback Mason Rudolf, then proceeded to whack Rudolf in the head with the very thing that was supposed to protect his skull.

This was followed by the hotheaded reaction of Browns defensive back Larry Ogunjobi, who jumped into the absurd altercation by punching and shoving Rudolf to the ground. Coming to Rudolf's defense, Steeler center Maurkice Pouncey jumped into Garrett, punching and kicking him.

With the loss of Garrett's temporary mental capacity, the Browns lost their Pro Bowl defensive end for the remainder of the season and possibly for a few games of the 2020 season. Furthermore, the Browns and the Steelers each had to pay $250,000 for their roles in this intolerable event.

After the game, Garrett told the media: "What I did was foolish, and I shouldn't allow myself to slip like that. That's out of character, but a situation like that where it's an emotional game, and I allowed myself to fall into those emotions with what happened."

INTENSITY	HAPPINESS	SADNESS	ANGER	FEAR	SHAME
HIGH	Elated Excited Overjoyed Thrilled Exuberant Ecstatic Fired up Passionate	Depressed Agonized Alone Hurt Dejected Hopeless Sorrowful Miserable	Furious Enraged Outraged Boiling Irate Seething Loathsome Betrayed	Terrified Horrified Scared stiff Petrified Fearful Panicky Frantic Shocked	Sorrowful Remorseful Defamed Worthless Disgraced Dishonored Mortified Admonished
MEDIUM	Cheerful Gratified Good Relieved Satisfied Glowing	Heartbroken Somber Lost Distressed Let down Melancholic	Upset Mad Defended Frustrated Agitated Disgusted	Apprehensive Frightened Threatened Insecure Uneasy Intimidated	Apologetic Unworthy Sneaky Guilty Embarassed Secretive
LOW	Glad Contented Pleasant Tender Pleased Mellow	Unhappy Moody Blue Upset Disappointed Dissatisfied	Perturbed Annoyed Uptight Resistant Irritated Touchy	Cautious Nervous Worried Timid Unsure Anxious	Bashful Ridiculous Regretful Uncomfortable Pitied Silly

FIGURE 1. This list outlines the common emotions that athletes experience. Copy these down or make your own list that you can refer to in the future.

What Your Emotions Mean

As an athlete, recognizing your emotions does not benefit you if you do not identify the reasons behind them. Think of your negative emotions as an alert system, indicating that you are reliving a past event or perceiving a possible future experience. The question you need to ask is, *What thought pattern led me to this emotional interruption?*

Here's an easy way to identify a negative thought pattern you may have while playing your sport—before an emotional response is generated.

If you are feeling angry or frustrated in the present moment, consider how this downward spiral began when you thought about or remembered something negative that had already happened. When you make a mistake while playing, where does that heightened emotional response come from? It's your in-the-moment reaction to the error, followed by thoughts from the past that you can't seem to let go of. You can only be angry or frustrated over a past event. There is nothing you can do now about the previous action that caused you to lose your cool, but you still cannot seem to mentally let go of the blunder. It's important to know, however, that by holding on to this, you're negatively affecting your ability to do what's needed in the present moment.

Feeling anxious or overwhelmed? This should tell you that you're projecting your thoughts into the future about a needed outcome. Or worse, you're thinking about a possible failed experience that has not even occurred yet. Many players will typically do this the night before a match or tournament. They will visualize the worst-case scenario, or they will churn over the "what-ifs" for hours instead of getting a solid night's sleep.

When you arrive for the event, you may instantly start overanalyzing the game you're about to play. This will cause you to begin to feel anxious or apprehensive. An even more detrimental circumstance would be possibly moving into fight or flight mode. Either way, by not staying in the present moment and being consciously aware of what emotions you're currently experiencing, you're setting yourself up for an avoidable disappointment—even though the game has not yet begun.

Before we learn how to grasp what self-regulation is and how to incorporate it into your game, I want you to understand another very important reason a player will have a heightened response before and/or while playing their sport.

StillPoint Insight #2.

After you have screwed up while playing your sport, decide how you could have done it differently and then move on!

Understanding Your Instinctive Emotional Response to Emotional Memories

Every athlete has had experiences they would love to forget; these are called emotional memories. Emotional memories can cause athletes to react automatically based on events from the past. Whether it was a major loss, injury, or a mental collapse that occurred, there is always one, if not a few, that would be best forgotten. One of the best skills an athlete can have is a short-term memory.

Imagine if on the first day of a golf tournament you had overreached and tried to drive past a water hazard, landing in the pond. That mistake really gets in your head. Dwelling on this error while approaching that hole in round two could have catastrophic results unless you can find a way to exorcise the memory.

However, our brains were created to do the exact opposite. Our mind's only objective is survival at all costs. Your brain must remember anything that caused you pain or mental anguish in the past so that you will never repeat that action again.

In order for this to happen, God (or whatever higher power you believe in) helped us evolve from cavemen by giving us what is known as the amygdala.

Your amygdala consists of two almond-shaped clusters of cells located inside your head, at the base of your brain. It plays a big part in your ability to feel emotions, such as fear and anxiety. Some have labeled these glands "your threat center." This is where your emotions are remembered as well as the response you had to them.

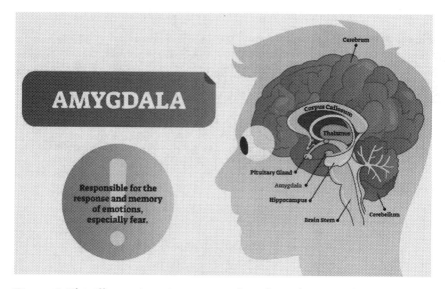

Figure 2 This illustration gives you an idea where the Amygdala is located.

If you feel mentally or physically threatened in any way, your amygdala is working on your behalf. It identifies perceived threats in microseconds.

When you are in extreme danger, your amygdala automatically reacts and sends your body into fight or flight mode. For example, when you are crossing a street and a car is flying toward you, without thinking you would instinctively jump or run to get out of the way. You would not stop and analyze how fast the car was moving. Your amygdala reacts immediately and disconnects your thinking process to save your life.

A tennis stroke coming at your head at 150 miles per hour? Your amygdala will tell you to duck, but in retrospect, putting your racquet up and defending the shot is a better response.

If you are coherent and know that you feel or may experience only a mild sense of risk or threat, then the prefrontal section of your brain overrides the amygdala and will help you make rational decisions on how to proceed.

However, if you are not consciously aware of your emotions or how an experience is affecting you, your amygdala will take over the driver's seat. In most cases, the consequences will be illogical choices and irrational thinking, with the result always being regret or embarrassment.

Your amygdala also stores the memories of any past harmful or heartbreaking experiences. Your brain will proceed to attach significance to the emotional memory based on the magnitude of emotions that were associated with it. These memories could be from either a physical experience you have encountered or an exceedingly emotional occurrence you may have had. Your brain only knows something has happened that caused you to have an extreme negative emotional response. Therefore, it will safeguard you at any expense necessary by remembering every detail about the event so it doesn't happen again.

This supposed threat does not have to be an identical occurrence; it could be an experience of a similar nature or even indirectly related to what happened previously. Yet a sudden remembrance or reaction activates within us so fast that the brain does not have time to process what the differences may be.

Without warning, we suddenly react by getting fearful, anxious, or even angry—feelings that are triggered by the imprinted memory of the past situation.

In order for the brain to accomplish this, it has to take a snapshot of the experience by using your five physical senses: sight, smell, taste, hearing, and touch.

This in-the-moment snapshot captures what you saw around you, the sounds you were hearing, and anything else that would be relevant in helping to warn you in the future of a reoccurrence of this unwanted or traumatic event.

If there is an experience that an athlete knows will set off this response, the best way to tackle it is head-on. Think back and identify what caused this fear or hesitation to begin with. However, do not overanalyze the cause; these doubts usually boil down to one specific origin. Once you identify it, you realize the anxiety you're feeling has nothing to do with the event that is happening now. Acknowledge that while this apprehension feels genuine to you, you have the ability to bring yourself back into alignment in this current moment, and not let it risk your athletic performance.

Imagine the pitcher who accidentally beaned a batter, perhaps seriously injuring him, and is now challenged to throw strikes consistently with this stuck in the forefront of his mind.

If this is something you are struggling with and you are not able to overcome this barrier, I suggest you find a mental coach who can work with you and help you finally put it to rest.

I am a firm believer that any disadvantage that you once had can be overcome and, in turn, become an advantage to your mental and physical game in the future.

CHAPTER 2

Learning How to Emotionally Self-Regulate

The time when there is no one there to feel sorry for you or to cheer for you is when a player is made.

-Tim Duncan

In the world we live in today, it is virtually impossible to have only positive emotions, much less sustain positive emotions throughout your entire day. But that is exactly what I am asking you to do. Not only will it help you be a happier person, someone people will enjoy spending their time with, but your level of game will also significantly increase. Here are a few benefits of positive emotions:

increased longevity
increased resilience to adversity
increased cognitive flexibility
increased memory
increased immune function
increased problem solving
increased intuition and creativity

Self-regulation is the practice of bringing yourself back to a centered state of mind and not letting your emotional reaction get the best of you. (I never understood why this saying was worded this way. A better way to state this would be, "getting the worst of you.") My son, Bouldin, likes to say, "Since you have 86,400 seconds in a day, why would you let a moment that lasted 400 seconds wreck your day?"

I would like to explain a scientifically proven concept that will help take you to a coherent state or bring you back to one after an emotional spiral has taken place. But first let us talk about one specific emotion.

There are many positive emotions such as excitement, passion, enthusiasm, joy, and optimism. However, my favorite emotion is appreciation—it is the awareness of unconditional enjoyment.

Appreciation is the emotion you feel when you are in the presence of something or someone that lights you up with joy for no other reason than just being there. You can also feel appreciation when you are somewhere beautiful, in a place that engulfs you in peace and serenity and where your only job is to relax and unwind.

Those are two great examples of this emotion. But even so, there are many ways to find instances to feel appreciation. If you were to stop and look around right now, you would find something to be pleased about. Perhaps it is where you are sitting. Or it simply could be appreciating that you have this moment to yourself right now.

I know it may seem that I am getting soft here, but there is a reason for me to explain the emotion of appreciation more fully in detail to you. So stay with me here a little longer. And no, I will not be asking you to see the world through rose-colored glasses or see life with no objectivity.

I do believe that people are starting to take the time to look around and acknowledge all the amazing things in life to be grateful for. For what I am about to explain, I feel it would be more beneficial to practice appreciation rather than looking for things to be grateful for.

It is common to interchange appreciation with gratitude, and I can see why it would be easy to do so. When you are grateful for someone or something, there is a sense of owing something in return for what was offered—the sense of being obliged to repay what was done for you. For example, take a look at the following comments:

> *I am really grateful for the help you gave me.*
> *I really appreciate the help you gave me.*
>
> *I am truly grateful for the gift you have given me.*
> *I truly appreciate the gift you have given to me.*

The impression you sense when using the word "appreciation" feels more unconditional, whereas the term "grateful" suggests needing to do something in return for what was offered.

Appreciation is being mindfully present in the moment and acknowledging the enjoyment of whatever has your current attention. If you would then accentuate that positive thought by taking in all the details surrounding it, your mind will naturally build upon it with like-minded thoughts.

Think of the feeling you have when you walk into your home and that four-legged creature is running toward you and wagging its tail. You begin to instantly light up and relax, while all the concerns you had before walking into the door seem to melt away. There are very few things in life we have unconditional love for, so when we see or experience them, they will grab and hold our undivided attention. Pets fall into this category because they want nothing from you in return for their love other than food and the occasional butt scratch.

The reason I have been rattling on about appreciation is because this emotion has a direct link to your clear coherent thinking and decision-making process (otherwise known as the zone or the flow state).

When you think of emotions, think of them as energy in action. You are activating the energy in and around your body, energy that not only can you physically sense, but that can also be felt by the people and the opponents around you.

Think of the emotion shown when a basketball player nails a buzzer beater at the end of a quarter. That positive rush is palpable by his teammates, and likely just as deflating for the opponents.

The energy of your heightened emotions starts in your heart and then communicates to your brain what physical and chemical response should be taken in reaction to your current feelings.

For several years now, I have had the pleasure of being affiliated with the HeartMath ® Institute. This nonprofit was founded in 1991 by Doc Childre to examine the heart and its role in the human system.

When HeartMath® Institute first began, the objective was to see if it could find any link between the heart and people's emotional state. After experimenting with many methods using an ECG (electrocardiogram), the institute discovered that the pattern of the heart rhythm reflected a person's emotional state better than any other test done previously.

HeartMath® Institute also looked at the heart rate (number of times the heart beats in a minute) and the heart rate variability (called HRV—the variation in the time between heart beats). What it found was that emotions did change the HRV. The institute concluded that the pattern of beat-to-beat variations showed changes in the emotional state. These findings were published in the *American Journal of Cardiology* in 1995 by McCraty and colleagues.

Their research determined that heartening emotions such as appreciation, joy, and love create a fluid heart-rhythm pattern. However, the reactions of negative feelings, such as anger, frustration, and anxiety, produce jagged, sharp heart-rhythm patterns.

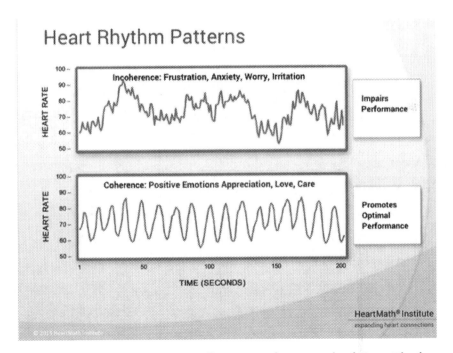

Figure 3 A HeartMath® Institute illustration of an example of Heart Rhythm Patterns.

Furthermore, HeartMath® Institute discovered that positive emotions produce a smooth HRV, creating higher brain functions. Research shows that the following effects of positive emotions are

- the ability to think clearly;
- the power to enhance your performance;
- the gift of optimal physical coordination;
- the capability to be decisive;
- the facility to generate intuitive problem-solving methods.

Have you ever noticed when you are angry that you cannot seem to think clearly? You may even begin to say things that you do not mean to express. Or perhaps you recall playing in a game when you had no conscious awareness of the time or score. You possibly experienced confusion as to why your performance or whatever physical action you were attempting was off its mark, yet you believed you were performing it correctly.

It's like the golfer who keeps slicing their drives yet believes their mechanics are spot on. It's quite possible they're simply mentally distracted by the anger they felt earlier when another golfer trash-talked them about their performance the previous day. It may be completely unconscious, but that anger is prohibiting them from thinking clearly on the course.

Now think back to a time when your performance just seemed to flow perfectly. You were so dialed in to the present moment that everything felt effortless, and all your physical senses were fully locked in and activated.

If you could now try to remember the moments leading up to that particular flow experience, you would probably recall being at ease, being in the moment of mindful awareness. And my guess is you were (consciously or not) appreciating your surroundings and loving in that moment, playing the sport you have spent countless hours performing.

How the Heart and Brain Connects

When most athletes are about to compete, they can experience heightened emotional reactions. These emotions affect their ANS (autonomic nervous system). An increased heart rate is the first clue you are about to create an imbalance in your nervous system.

The ANS functions on a subconscious level. It is also heavily involved with the ability to feel and experience emotions, and it controls a majority of bodily functions.

Most people believe that their emotions are mental expressions stemming from the mind. We now know this is not to be the case. Your emotions are reflected in your heart, communicated to the brain, and then responded to by the body. And it is your autonomic nervous system that connects the heart, brain, and body.

The autonomic nervous system carries signals from your heart to your brain center and vice versa. The unexpected discovery here, though, is that your heart communicates to your brain more so than the brain to the heart.

As I discussed earlier, your heart sends a signal to the brain and has a profound influence on your mental capacities. These signals are like the Morse code, developed in the nineteenth century as a form of communication. Nerve impulses from the heart signal to the brain whatever your current emotion is. Whether you are feeling appreciation or experiencing stress, your heart is communicating to the brain what you are presently experiencing. So how does your ANS work?

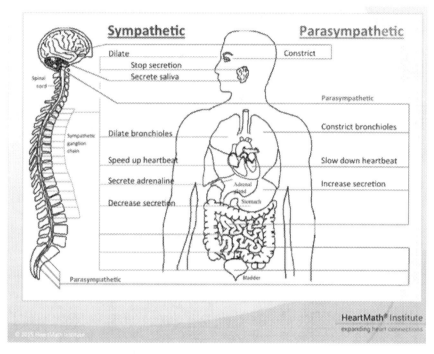

Figure 4 A HeartMath® Institute illustration of the Autonomic Nervous System.

Your autonomic nervous system has two branches. One branch is the sympathetic nervous system, which prepares the body for action by speeding up the heart rate.

The other branch is the parasympathetic nervous system, which is tasked with slowing down your heart rate. To help visualize this, think of the sympathetic branch as being the gas pedal in a car and the parasympathetic branch being the brake pedal.

When you are feeling anger or frustration, it is as if you were driving with one foot on the gas and the other foot on the brake pedal simultaneously. Your car would be jerking you around to the point of whiplash. Basically, it would jolt you back and forth from not knowing what you want from it.

Well, that is exactly what you are signaling to your brain when you have let your emotions get the best (worst) of you.

Anxiety, anger, and frustration cause the signals in the nervous system to become erratic and, as a result, will drive you into fight or flight mode. However, the emotion of appreciation reflects an increased synchronization in the autonomic nervous system and moves you into a heightened conscious state.

I teach my clients to shift gears back into a coherent mindset after they have let the ball drop, so to speak, by using the HeartMath® Institute's quick coherence technique, which I'll explain in this section.

Remember, by having alignment with your heart and brain, your reaction times, coordination, and situational awareness improve dramatically. Not only will you have improved long- and short-term memory, your ability to focus, solve problems, and make the appropriate decisions will be self-evident. There is no reason for you to not do this for yourself today. As an elite athlete, you're willing to do whatever it takes to improve your physical game; I am suggesting you do the same for your mental game.

Before I instruct you on this simple yet effective technique, I need for you to choose a mental image that you will be using as your appreciation visual. As suggested earlier, I recommend your visual be a pet you have or have known, a special animal that made you light up every time you saw them.

Or the visual can be of a place where you found peace and a sense of balance simply by being in that setting. Please do not picture anyone being with you in this mental image; this will now be your private setting where you can always go to realign yourself.

You might be wondering why I have not suggested a human loved one for your appreciation visual. We all have a loved one or child we feel an unconditional love for. However, depending on the day or that moment in time, we might not be feeling very unconditional toward that particular person. As much as I love my son, and most of the time feel as if he could do no wrong, there will always be occasions when we push one another's buttons. So, for the sake of your own stability, I suggest having this visual be about yourself or a loving pet.

In order to employ an effective visualization technique, you must use your five physical senses to bring this image to life with clarity. Sense the feeling of the grainy sand in between your toes or imagine the warmth of the sand on your fingers. Remember how soft or rough your pet's fur is. Bring to mind the sounds of the waves crashing on the beach or remind yourself of the sounds coming from your four-legged best friend running to you as you walk in the door. Smell the salty ocean air surrounding you or recall the questionable breath coming from the mouth of your unconditionally loved pet.

By using your five senses, you are pulling that memory or imagery into your real-time consciousness. Draw in enough of the emotion so it is felt, seen, smelled, tasted, or heard in the forefront of your mind; the brain will not know if it is being actualized in reality or being pulled from a stored memory.

Now hold this vision with the physical senses in play for twenty seconds, until you have imprinted it into your memory bank. You will be using this visual for the technique I will be describing or anytime you need to pull yourself back into mental alignment. Once you have practiced and set this visual into your mind numerous times, you can summon the imprinted image whenever it is needed.

The quick coherence technique is used to bring yourself out of a heightened emotion and self-regulate you back into a coherent mindset. It can be used before a demanding workout or before playing your sport—whenever you need to bring your focus back into the present moment so that you can harness your emotional response.

It is about slowing down the mental and emotional reactions that are causing mistakes and impulsive reactions. *You are creating a mental StillPoint of the mind while being on the move.*

QUICK COHERENCE TECHNIQUE

Step 1: **Focus your attention on the area of your heart. Imagine your breath is flowing in and out of your heart or chest area, breathing a little slower and deeper than usual. Find an easy rhythm that's comfortable.**

Step 2: **As you continue heart-focused breathing, make a sincere attempt to experience a regenerative feeling such as appreciation or care for someone or something in your life.**

Additional Suggestions for the Technique

If you are having a hard time centering your attention in this area, place your hand or finger in the center of your chest and gently tap. As an added benefit, the physical sensation of tapping on this focal point will help you to stay in the present moment.

As you focus on the area of your heart, feel your chest rise and fall with each inhalation. Imagine your breath is flowing in and out through your heart. Slowly breathe into the count of five and then slowly breathe out to a count of five. Do this until your breathing feels smooth and balanced. As you continue to breathe with ease for a few moments, you will find a natural inner rhythm that feels right. I would also like to suggest that when you are exhaling, that you release the tension from your shoulders. Feel your shoulders begin to drop each time you exhale. This will help release any tension that might have built up.

Once you have completed these steps, Bring back your visual of appreciation into your mind's eye. *Please do not forget to enhance the remembrance using your five senses.*

Continue to breathe through the area of your heart and begin to feel the positive emotions that you invoke from experiencing that heart-felt connection you have with the pet or place that you love unconditionally.

To learn more about HeartMath® Institute and the techniques they use, visit **www.heartmath.org**.

Tips

1. Before going into a future event, take inventory of those past negative experiences where you know that you will likely be triggered. This is so you will be aware of the possible memory and you can anticipate the reaction that might occur. For instance, the tennis player who gets frustrated competing against left-handers needs to mentally adjust so it does not become an ongoing issue. Now that you know that it is not fear behind this trigger—it is just your brain supporting your

survival by any means necessary—you can quickly move past this glitch in your performance.

2. Take inventory of your best performances and wins and let them fuel your ego when needed.

3. Set your intentions before going into any new segment of your day. By knowing what your focused intent is, you will be more likely to stay on track with what you want to accomplish, and less likely to be weighed down with wasted heightened emotions. I will discuss this more later in the book.

4. Use your five physical senses to keep you in the present moment while playing your sport. Feel the wind on your face. Feel your feet as you walk to take a break or as you are walking to your next objective. Feel the weight or the texture of whatever sporting equipment you use. Find a focal point to look at, whether it is something you are wearing or an object that is in front of you.

Read the words that are on your water bottle when you take a break. Or watch and be aware of your movements as you are regrouping for your play. Hear your breath as you are slowly exhaling through parted lips.

CHAPTER 3

Becoming Resilient to Stress and Adversity

Passion first and everything will fall into place.

-Holly Ham

A characteristic trait of every great athlete is the ability to be resilient against stress and adversity. Being resilient means possessing the capacity to prepare for, recover from, and adapt in the face of stress, adversity, or change beyond our control.

A few signs that an athlete may need to build more resiliency in their game are

- constantly overanalyzing their performance;
- self-talking negatively internally or externally;
- feeling weighed down or freezing altogether from the feeling of being overwhelmed;
- becoming easily distracted;
- reacting to the opponent versus focusing on their own appropriate maneuver;
- making excuses for not being able to give it their all.

Being resilient means you can turn adversity into a challenge that you can look forward to.

The golfer who is suddenly struggling with their short game and is starting to get tense every time they pull their wedge or putter out needs to remember this part of the game can be fun. Once they embrace that challenge and get excited about chipping and putting again, that slump will soon be over.

StillPoint Insight #3

Athletes who perceive adversity as a mountain they have to climb will not have the mental capacity to sustain what it will take to overcome the journey.

Players might find themselves no longer challenged in their sport. They might have begun settling into a predictable level of competition for an extended period of time. If they then suddenly find themselves playing in a higher level of competition they are more likely to find themselves falling into the fight or flight syndrome trap (or what I like to call Freeze, Fight or Flight).

A player could either freeze mentally or physically; in other words, they can experience a panic attack. (In 2018, Cleveland Cavaliers forward Kevin Love candidly admitted to dealing with this very issue, and his panic attack occurred right in the middle of a game.) Or an athlete will try to fight their way through it, which leads to them merely reacting to the opponent. And there is flight. When this happens players will have the tendency to avoid or make excuses to not meet the challenges head-on in the future.

However, if you can see adversity as an opportunity to learn and build resilience, you are one step closer to becoming the athlete you want to become.

Your perception of the challenge in front of you is what determines the outcome in your game. It is your choice how you will decide to view your life's difficult situations whenever they arise. And from that perspective, you will have two very different responses to the circumstance.

In some instances, a player might have what I like to call a "defying response." This response plays out when an athlete aspires to take on any unexpected difficulty that comes their way and to overcome it or learn from the experience no matter what the end result is. The elite athlete knows that if he does this, it will never blindside him again and can't become a weakness in the future.

I ask my clients to write down any disadvantages they feel are hindering their game. I also have the client create a list of any distractions they have noticed getting in their way. One by one, I will show them how to embrace and overcome each disadvantage or distraction.

StillPoint Insight #4

Every apparent disadvantage or hardship you
face head-on will make you stronger. You can
then use it to your advantage in the future.

The second response is not a conscious choice, but an automatic response the body will have when the athlete's brain believes it may be in danger.

This is the "fight or flight syndrome." This is the body's automatic response to acute stress. The heart's pounding response to the stress signals to the brain that the athlete is in duress. The same response would occur if the player were about to experience physical harm outside of the game.

As mentioned in Chapter One, fight or flight is a survival mechanism we were born with. This response not only keeps us safe from danger but helps us to remember the danger, so that we will steer clear of similar experiences in the future.

Here are a few of physical signs that you may experience when you find yourself unknowingly exhibiting fight or flight syndrome:

- Your heart begins to race
- Your mouth goes dry
- Your muscles tense up
- Your breath starts to quicken
- Your body produces more sweat than needed
- Your balance is shaken
- Your thoughts and words become incoherent

Those are some of the noticeable physical signs you will experience. However, there is one side effect to fight or flight that is not noticeable, and that is the stress hormone cortisol that is being released into your body.

I will be writing about this fight or flight response and cortisol in detail in the following chapter. I will be also going over the main chemicals that shoot through your system in reaction to many of your daily positive emotions.

What to Do

No matter what sport you play or how much stability you may feel in your life, there will always be things you feel you have no control over. I believe this benefits the mind, as without these uncontrollable situations you would never become more than you are right now.

Some recreational players think it is desirable to avoid difficult challenges. We are all familiar with the adult recreational sports in which players are more than happy to stay with the handicap or level they are currently at for the repeated wins rather than challenging themselves and competing at their true level. However, this doesn't work for the athlete who wants to advance.

StillPoint Insight #5

In order for you to dominate your mental and emotional game, you must remember that it is always your choice how you respond to what life throws at you.

Here are some of my suggestions for building your resilience and gaining power over uncontrollable events.

1. <u>Make a list</u> of whatever it is that you feel you have no control over in a particular category in your life. It may be at school, at home, or in your sport. Then write down what, within your power, you can do about that category to make the outcome better for you. Here is a timely example that occurred just as I was making final tweaks on the book during the 2020 coronavirus pandemic.

Quarantine

No control over:

- I have no control over when we will be allowed to play our sport again.
- I am not allowed to practice with my teammates during this time.
- I was not able to attend any showcases this year because of the quarantine.

Things in my power that I can do now:

- I can level up my workouts to increase my strength for next season.
- I can hold myself accountable for my own drills and my own individual practices.
- I can read articles or watch videos on YouTube that will better my performance when the sport returns.
- I can take advantage of this time to better myself and my performance to get ahead of my opponents who might not be using this time to benefit themselves.

2. Be aware of and acknowledge everything that you do right! Take time in every part of your day to acknowledge something great that you have accomplished or mastered.

In an average day, everyone has roughly five different memorable things that happen. Now, there may be days that are more notable and some that are not so mind-blowing. However, out of those give-or-take five experiences, more of them will be good and one or two will be great. However, at the end of the day most people will generally chew over the one negative experience that did not go their way. Why is that? I believe it is our brain's way of doing recon and planning an attack for the next time this negative experience arises.

If I go along with this line of thinking, I believe we should consciously look at what did not go our way, decide how we can learn from the experience, and then plan a strategy to take it on headfirst if the situation ever does show its ugly face again. But here is the most important part: let it go afterwards!

Spend the rest of your evening reflecting, remembering the laughs you may have had. Or commit to memory the athletic performance that you nailed that day. Let those images be the last experiences you think of as you close your eyes and fall asleep.

3. <u>Appreciate</u> the life you have now. Where you are right now is the culmination of the choices you have made up until this point. Whether they were great choices or decisions you wish you could erase from your memory, appreciate the fact you have a choice right now on how you will live your life today.

Take a moment when you first wake up in the morning and appreciate the soft bed you are lying in. Do not reflect on this for too long or you will fall right back to sleep. (I know this from experience!) If you have a loved one or a pet lying beside you, spend a few moments appreciating that they are there.

If your mind starts dwelling on the day's to-do list, *stop* and recognize that you already know what is on your calendar. Do not begin to project any opinions or fears based on past events on today's schedule. Concede that you truly have no idea how those events will turn out.

From my earliest memories, I recall being an optimist. I was always looking for the bright side of most situations. As I matured, I began seeing the benefits of the challenges I faced.

On the one hand, I was the daydreamer who saw everything through rose-colored glasses, but on the other hand, I was visualizing how I could gain the upper hand to benefit from the various circumstances I had to go up against.

Understanding how the heart and brain work together in unison not only brings you the knowledge of the flow state. It also takes you to the next level because you are able to see challenges as possible benefits for you.

Having resiliency is not just about making it through difficult situations. It means realizing the advantage you can obtain from them. Every human being on this planet hates losing, but it is the clever person who will put their loss into perspective and gain insight from the occasional defeat.

Realize and admit physical deficiencies and add or adjust workout routines. Recognize the game tactics that need to be improved upon to be able to tackle this same style of opponent the next time. Become aware of any mental setbacks that are hindering your game.

Jennifer Heistand

I wrote the following article some time ago for Florida Tennis Magazine. See if it resonates with how you would like to live your life.

I Don't Know, a New Perspective

When we say "I don't know" to all of the things we thought we previously knew or believed in, it is liberating to the mind. It relinquishes control of the subconscious mind and hands it over to the conscious one.

The conscious mind is the one that is focused on the present moment. The one that can see an experience for how it truly is. The conscious mind does not rely on past experiences or previously held beliefs to direct its attention. It is the one that is focused on your life that is playing out in front of you right now. Your conscious mind is life itself unfolding before your eyes.

This mind is free to form its own opinion and perspective based what you see with a clear lens that has no filters upon it that you might have had on the previous day—such as a blind man might do when suddenly opening his eyes for the first time and seeing vibrant colors, instead of the lifeless colors he had imagined based on the opinions of what other well-intentioned people had told him that colors looked and felt like.

I am suggesting that at the beginning of your day when most people normally start assuming how their day is going to play out based on what the previous day brought to them, you stop yourself and say "I don't know". Start your day with a new assumption, one that says I do not have any idea what this day will bring me but I cannot wait to find out!

Jennifer Heistand

I wrote the following article some time ago for Florida Tennis Magazine. See if it resonates with how you would like to live your life.

I Don't Know, a New Perspective

When we say "I don't know" to all of the things we thought we previously knew or believed in, it is liberating to the mind. It relinquishes control of the subconscious mind and hands it over to the conscious one.

The conscious mind is the one that is focused on the present moment. The one that can see an experience for how it truly is. The conscious mind does not rely on past experiences or previously held beliefs to direct its attention. It is the one that is focused on your life that is playing out in front of you right now. Your conscious mind is life itself unfolding before your eyes.

This mind is free to form its own opinion and perspective based what you see with a clear lens that has no filters upon it that you might have had on the previous day—such as a blind man might do when suddenly opening his eyes for the first time and seeing vibrant colors, instead of the lifeless colors he had imagined based on the opinions of what other well-intentioned people had told him that colors looked and felt like.

I am suggesting that at the beginning of your day when most people normally start assuming how their day is going to play out based on what the previous day brought to them, you stop yourself and say "I don't know". Start your day with a new assumption, one that says I do not have any idea what this day will bring me but I cannot wait to find out!

This new perspective opens your eyes and views the world to be fresh and exciting, where there is no end to the possibilities of what life can show you. This perspective helps you see characteristics of life that you may have prejudged before based on tired beliefs that you have held onto and no longer benefit you.

Leave your mind to be curious and interested, like a child reading a book for the first time and experiencing a new adventure. You might be surprised at what you will find out about yourself and the people you interact with.

I am asking you to give your subconscious mind a break and let go of your preconceived ideas and beliefs about people and circumstances that you come in contact with, even if it is just for one day. Go into each interaction using your conscious mind and viewing the experience with a clear lens to see how vibrant life can truly be. Life is more interesting that way!

CHAPTER 4

The Five Main Chemicals That Affect Your Mind and Body

Ability is what you're capable of doing. Motivation determines what you do. Attitude determines how well you do it.

–Lou Holtz

You produce great chemicals throughout your body every day, and each one has a specific job to do. Depending on your emotions or needs, which are unique to everyone, certain chemicals will be released when you have a particular emotion or to reward you when a certain function has been carried out:

Dopamine helps motivate you to seek out rewards.
Endorphins help you to ignore pain.
Serotonin raises your confidence.
Oxytocin facilitates love and social bonds with others.
Cortisol alerts you to physical or mental pain.

As an athlete, you might be wondering why you need to understand the chemicals in your body and the reactions you have to them.

The reason is that the chemicals listed above are tied to your habits and thought patterns. Once you have the awareness and understanding of how they perform, you will be empowered to make them work for you. Everyone's bodies and brains are unique, and while the contents of our minds may be different, the fundamental nature of how these chemicals perform is the same.

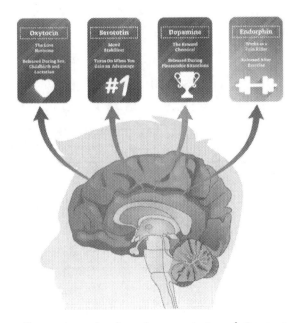

Figure 5 An illustration of a few characteristics of Oxytocin, Serotonin, Dopamine and Endorphin.

Other than the self-starters who come out of the womb wanting to take on the world, humans are basically lazy. So, for the rest of humanity, nature gave them motivators disguised as chemicals to allow them to survive and accomplish whatever it is that they want to do. And each one of these chemicals is triggered based on an activity the person is doing or the emotion they are feeling at that moment.

The Straight Dope with Dopamine

Dopamine is the chemical that shoots through your system whenever you feel as if you have done something amazing. Just sunk a winning shot or made a perfect line drive down the fairway? Dopamine is behind that feeling of *I did it!* Everyone can relate to that feeling of everything lining up perfectly. A light from the heavens is shining down upon you and an action you performed or expressed was nailed perfectly. So now that we've experienced perfection and know what it feels like, what do we do? We get back up the next day and work even harder to experience that feeling again. Dopamine is genius!

StillPoint Insight #6

It is the pursuit of the accomplishment that
ignites our fuel and feels so good.

Let's say you just wrapped up your workout and the idea pops in your head that you are getting hungry. Okay, your body is trying to tell you that it needs fuel. The brain tells the body to drop a little incentive. Drip, drip. Without that dopamine drip giving you that incentive, you might turn your attention to something else. When you finally listen to your famished body and follow through with what your stomach wanted, your taste buds come alive with the first bite. You savor that simple bite as if it were the best thing you have ever put into your mouth. Poof! Your brain just shot you with dopamine again as a reward for following through with what the body needed.

Depending on the size of the task that you want to accomplish and the level of anticipation you feel to complete it, your brain will release enough dopamine to keep you motivated until you finish what you have started.

Each of your tasks or aspirations has one or more possible rewards attached to it. It does not matter if it is a material reward, social reward, or even an internal high-five. They all have dopamine attached to them.

Athletes will spend countless hours training and working out because dopamine encourages them each day with an internal high-five. The athlete knows that with each drop of sweat that drips down their forehead, they are one step closer to achieving their goal. With the dopamine reward motivating the athlete to push themselves harder to train more than the next guy to be successful, you can see why dopamine is so important.

For an athlete, these goals are even clearer, given the vast statistical means in which sports are measured.

All chemicals being released in your body are based on cause and effect. We unassumingly receive this chemical each time we move toward a goal that we have set out for ourselves. It's ultimately combined with a larger dose as an incentive when we have accomplished it, but then we sober up and the prize goes away. If the chemical did not have a stop button, what would make us want to go again?

If you would like to experience more dopamine in your life, here are a few ways to get it.

If you have a *physical* to-do list (which I suggest is a good idea for everyone, ideally placed where it can be seen), take the time to cross off each accomplishment, no matter how small it is, before diving into the next dreaded scribbled task. The sense of accomplishment feels good, so take a second to physically cross off the chore that you wrote down, even if it is something as easy as finally calling your mom back!

Once you start noticing how rewarding if feels to shorten your daily to-do list, start up another one. One that has *Goals That Will be Achieved* written on top.

You spend more than ten minutes every day daydreaming about what you would rather be doing versus the work in front of you. So spend those ten minutes writing down one goal, along with several steps or ideas about how this desire can be realized. Just penciling down a future goal that you have been thinking about, along with some ideas on how to make it possible, will give you a blast of dopamine. This desired goal has not come out of thin air, it has been noodling around in your head for some time now. So as an added benefit, it will clear some space in your mind that you need to focus your attention on what is required right now.

Meet Your Endorphins

One of the first basic incentives that was given to us was endorphins. Endorphins mask the pain initially brought on by physical injury so we can survive or get away if needed, much like how doctors give us morphine when we are experiencing severe pain. If a caveman mistakenly clubbed his own foot while fighting off a saber-toothed tiger, it was the endorphins being signaled from the brain that kicked into his system, allowing the caveman to hurriedly limp away.

It is no coincidence that when endorphins were first discovered, they were called endogenous morphine, because morphine acted quite similarly to our own bodies' natural defense to pain.

It is this chemical that explains how a tennis player can painfully twist an ankle, then somehow get up and not only grit their way through another set-and-a-half of play but emerge victorious.

We have all experienced endorphins in some form or another. This neurochemical is the euphoric high you get during an extreme workout. The time it takes for the endorphins to kick in varies based on the level or impact of workout you are engaged in. When they do kick in, you will know it. Your body feels lighter and you feel stronger, able to take on whatever challenge you set up for yourself.

Imagine your body releasing a sigh of relief because you have finally reached the stage of your workout when your body goes on autopilot and you don't have to try as hard to achieve your natural pace. You are not making excuses as to why you can shorten your workout and grab a smoothie. You're now thinking you might even tack on some extra training today. You're on fire!

The problem comes when reality sets in later in the day. Our bodies are not built withstand pain for long periods of time. Endorphins will only get you through your workout and the initial bout of pain that you are subjecting yourself to.

After the workout, whether you are back in a classroom or trying to relax at home, you are going to experience pain. This is when your muscles and tendons sober up from the endorphin high. You wish you could receive a morphine drip but you settle for Advil.

The funny thing is, the very next day you want to get right back out there and do it all over again. We crave the high that only endorphins can give us. Not to mention the fact that our ego is being fed by how great our body looks and the feeling of vitality coursing through our veins. And it feels satisfying to know that we did not give ourselves a free pass on the day's promised workout. Which leads me to the next chemical I want to discuss, serotonin.

But first, I want to include other ways to experience endorphins without having to inflict intentional pain upon ourselves. One is to laugh—whether that is laughing at yourself, which I highly recommend-or laughing with friends. Laugh so hard that you are holding back tears and your abs hurt from the internal convulsions taking place in your stomach. Those convulsions are signaling to your intellect that you are in distress. So not only are you getting that rare belly laugh; you are also receiving the *feel no pain* chemical that every athlete desires.

If you typically work out several days a week but yet have not been experiencing the same level of endorphins that you have in the past, then change up your routine. In general, if a person does not have a professional trainer guiding them through their routine, they will have a tendency to work the same muscles or areas of their body repeatedly. So, if you want to rekindle your relationship with endorphins, give some of your other muscles or body parts a spot in the limelight. You will not have to work out as long or as hard as your previous routine since these newbie muscles have not experienced the strain as your previously overworked muscles have, so the rush will kick in a lot sooner.

Rekindle Your Pride with Serotonin

All you athletes out there, here is a chemical for you. As I mentioned earlier, serotonin is the chemical that kicks in your ego. Serotonin fills you with pride. It gave prehistoric people the confidence to win the most desirable mates. It makes you want to pound your chest and say *I am the greatest!* This is very important for an athlete; you absolutely need to have an ego if you are to excel. If an athlete does not have 100 percent confidence in themselves, they will not be successful.

> StillPoint Insight #7
>
> It is an evolutionary urge to want to be at the top
> of our game and to have the competitive edge.

Every human being wants to feel secure, and serotonin helps us to create a sense of security *within ourselves*. The human brain is constantly monitoring its surroundings to find evidence that it can use to blanket itself in with the assurance of warm snuggly thoughts to build our self-confidence. With the assistance of serotonin, we are persistently on the pursuit of looking for examples of our own greatness.

Serotonin doesn't only affect you, it also effects your parents, loved ones, and peers. As a mental coach to athletes, I have noticed all the great players want to make their parents and coaches proud. It forms a bond when there is pride involved; it is an ebb and flow of energy.

The feeling of pride demonstrates to the athletes that their parents and coaches believe in them and they want to prove that their supporters' belief was deserved. Here is an example: You have just accomplished the game-winning shot and you are on top of the world. You get your blast of serotonin, then you look up into the stands and there they are, looking at you with such pride and admiration. Because of the pride they are feeling, they are getting a shot of serotonin as well.

Regardless of whether you performed the amazing feat or someone else did, if you have feelings or emotions tied to that player, your body will react and respond in the same way as the athletes.

There are many other examples in your life that will demonstrate your self-worth and produce the same results.

Start noticing when you make decisions that have a positive impact on people's lives. Recognize even the smallest outcome from a choice you made that affected someone supportively. What decisions have you made in the past that supported someone and had a ripple effect on other people's lives?

Feeling pride in yourself reflects your sense of self-worth. There are many ways to demonstrate to yourself that you are worthy. If I accomplish three out of the four things on my to-do list, I will pound my chest and be proud of myself!

It is true that brains seek social dominance, but we crave social groupings and interactions with others as well. We want to trust that someone will have our back, whether it is believing in us or being there to fulfill a need. Which leads me to the next great chemical, one that's is released when we form bonds of trust.

Understanding Oxytocin

Oxytocin is the hormone that acts as a neurotransmitter and underlies individual and social trust. It creates social alliances and gives you a sense of belonging. As for the prehistoric humans, there was safety in numbers. I believe the cave dwellers received oxytocin to help them alleviate the suffocating feeling they must have had from being crammed into a dusky and obscure cave with their nearest and dearest. (Can you imagine the quarantine we just lived through without oxytocin?)

Oxytocin is the drug we feel coursing through our veins when we are in desperately in love. You can even experience oxytocin when you are shaking hands with someone. Of course, when you are in love with someone, you receive a tidal wave of oxytocin, but just get a drip from a handshake. However, even the smallest drip of this love drug will feel rewarding.

It has also been shown that when you witness an act of kindness, you will also receive this compassionate drug. I assume we were given this chemical to encourage our self-absorbed egos to do something nice for someone else. So all you athletes and leaders out there—the more you devote your time and energy to others less fortunate, the better you will feel. Literally!

I propose that you become more aware of the strangers you come across. Acknowledge them by looking at them and if appropriate, shake their hands. Just from those two simple gestures you will be rewarded with not only a better sense of your community, but you will get a jolt of oxytocin as well.

As a society, we have become more self-absorbed than ever. If for no other reason than to get rewarded with oxytocin, set your phone aside and notice the people you come into contact with.

If none of these suggestions tickle your fancy, here is one you might like. Go out and get a massage, something that also seems to stimulate oxytocin. You might find yourself in a better mindset to try one of the earlier suggestions.

Coming to Terms with Cortisol

The chemicals we just discussed are extremely important for our day-to-day lives. They help us understand what motivates and guides our daily habits and thoughts. These chemicals inspire us in times of need and support our self-confidence. However, the most significant chemical of all is cortisol, which is known as the stress hormone.

Cortisol is a chemical that is produced in times of stress. Depending on the level of stress that you are experiencing, your brain will determine the amount of cortisol it will give you. Your basic level of stress could be from just an overall bad day, a sudden argument with someone, or a tough loss in your sport.

The general effects are loss of sleep, fatigue, and loss of anti-inflammatory agents. However, elevated levels of cortisol over a prolonged period can and will result in the breaking down of proteins and lead to muscle wasting. (That's right, I said muscle wasting.) If you live in a continual state of stress or frustration, your body will start transporting potassium out of the cells of your bones. Elevated levels of cortisol also lengthen the recovery time needed to heal wounds or injuries. And we all know how important it is to get back in the game.

If all that is not bad enough, when you act out in extreme frustration or anger, your body will shoot out adrenaline along with cortisol. This helps to create a memory of this short-term emotional outburst or event, a situation called flashbulb memory. Your brain will assume that it is doing you a favor by creating a memory for you so it can remind you not to repeat whatever it was that caused the level of stress you experienced.

Your brain acts as a recorder, chronicling events that you are experiencing throughout the day. If the situation triggers cortisol, it will capture the moments leading up to it, using your five senses as a reference point.

Most people are familiar with veterans coming home from war who may have experienced unimaginable events. If these soldiers were exposed to a life-threatening situation in combat, they may experience post-traumatic stress disorder (PTSD), even after returning home to a safe environment. They will reexperience the trauma through flashbacks. Everything involved with the traumatic experience was recorded and downloaded for future reference, including the information that was picked up by the other four physical senses (smell, touch, taste and hearing). These veterans may avoid similar people, places, activities, or objects that would remind them of the event and trigger PTSD.

If a soldier were walking down a street with their family and heard a sudden blast of a noise—even as a loud horn—this could set off an exaggerated startled response based on the past experience. The brain will automatically alert the body that it is about to reexperience a traumatic event.

In the beginning, I believe we were given this chemical so that humans could avoid reexperiencing physical pain. If cavemen had no past memories, sensory imputes, or warnings signaling danger, they would never have survived. Our historical ancestors would have never remembered to not stick their hand into the fire to retrieve their meal. (It is amazing to me that we did survive at all!)

Cortisol truly is a benefit to us. Just imagine how much time you would spend daily trying to identify the next encounter that would cause you physical harm if you did not have this warning signal. And that's not just physical pain. How about emotional pain? Without cortisol's smack-in-the-back-of-the-head reminder, you would repeat the negative emotional experiences that you have already had to live through. Once you are reminded of what you do not want, you begin to learn what it is that you do want for your emotional needs.

Cortisol is your safety net. Thankfully, it stops you before making really bad decisions or, if you have already screwed up, cortisol will remind you in the future to not repeat the unfortunate choice you made in the past. (Cortisol is like your mother, who will never let you forget all the less-than-stellar ideas you previously had. Thanks, Mom!)

In any situation, your mind will search your memory bank for previous memories of times and events that are of a like-minded state. Basically, it will perform recon in order to help you out of the current situation. But if it is of the like-minded stressful nature, then you are just increasing your stress level and churning out more cortisol. And around and around you go. So, get off the memory-go-round and question whether whatever you are experiencing is really worth all that. (I would say 98 percent of it is not!)

Okay, so why was it that I wanted you to know about these five chemicals? It's called leverage! When you know what your body is capable of—and it is capable of so much, I assure you—you have leverage over your opponents. Once you begin to recognize where your mind is at and what is happening in your body at any given moment, there is nothing or no one that can stop you from being where you want to be.

CHAPTER 5

Finding Your Intrinsic and Extrinsic Motivation

An athlete cannot run with money in his pockets.
He must run with hope in his heart and dreams in
his head.

–Emil Zatopek

If you have motivation, you have a strong reason to act or accomplish something. It can come from internal or external clues.

If it is intrinsic, you have the desire to do something based on internal cues (e.g., enjoyment or interest). If it is extrinsic, you have the desire to do something based on external cues (e.g., to gain rewards or avoid consequences).

When I begin working with a client, one of the first questions I ask is, "Why do you love your sport?"

Love cannot be faked or forced. You either feel it or you don't. If you do not truly love your sport or can't identify what it is about your sport that drives you to want to succeed, you will never reach your full potential.

The importance of the connection you feel with your sport reveals to me not only what your motivation is but also helps me understand if you're performing for yourself or if you're performing for an external pressure, such as avoiding disapproval from your parents or peers.

If an athlete does not feel passion for the sport they are playing, one of two things may happen as a result. They will eventually quit playing the sport, or, even worse in my opinion— come to dread everything it takes to compete and begin to have mental resistance toward the challenges they will have to face. And if their head is not in the game, possible injuries can occur.

This is why it is very important to find your intrinsic and extrinsic motivation. I feel identifying both is essential to find your genuine connection to the sport.

As explained at the beginning of this chapter, there are two types of motivation that a player has for wanting to face competition. Intrinsic motivation comes into play when an athlete is motivated from personal gains such as improving themselves as a person or honing their skills. This drive may also come from wanting self-recognition; the player enjoys challenging himself, making himself feel confident. Or it may be a simple as just being in love with the game itself.

Extrinsic motivation is received from outside sources such as the desire for rewards, money, or attention. Who are we to judge what the driving force behind their ambitions are?

These are the most important questions I ask when I begin working with a client. It gives me insight about what motivates the athlete. It also is a reminder for them as to why they endure the physically demanding aspect of the sport. And more importantly, it is something I will be reminding them of each session, as I am reinforcing the mental aspect into their head.

In order to discover what motivates you, consider three factors: intimate reasoning, internal and external improvement, and a reason bigger than yourself.

Intimate reasoning determines knowing what your sport means to you and recognizing what it is that you personally gain from playing your sport.

Ask yourself *Why do I love competing in my sport? What do I intimately gain by playing?*

For these questions, usually the first answer that will pop into your mind will be the truthful response. There is no one around to judge your answer, even if the answer is *I'm damn good at it* or *I gain a lot of self-confidence by playing.*

That response would inform me that you are playing your sport for the benefit of feeling good, and that you care how you feel about yourself.

Your answer could be, *I love the feeling of belonging I get from playing my sport.* In a world where everyone seems to only be fixated on themselves, the sense of companionship and brotherhood is an aspect of sports that greatly benefits an athlete. It allows them to realize what it means to be held accountable to someone other than themselves.

A reason may be that you love the feeling of being part of a team and while you have an important part to play, the burden lies on everyone on the team to win. Or you might revel in the sense of camaraderie you receive as a group all striving for something together.

Other competitors enjoy the individualistic nature of a sport, such as golf or tennis. While these types of sports are mentally challenging, players have the benefit of having only to rely on themselves without the added stress of depending on teammates.

If you were to write down a list of reasons why you love competing in your sport and what you intimately gain from playing, you may find just one or two reasons, or the list may seem endless. What's most important is that you acknowledge and reaffirm these motives as often as possible.

For most, it is easy to forget why they love their sport when the game does not go their way. It's also difficult to recall that feeling when it seems too tough to keep pushing yourself to do what is necessary to be the best you can be. When these moments happen—and they will—remember to appreciate all of the positive aspects of the game and why it is so important to you.

Internal and External Improvement

If you as an athlete are improving in your physical game but still having resistance in your internal mental game, you will not have the perfect balance that is needed to maintain your competitive advantage.

There are many reasons why an athlete might find themselves feeling resistance in their mindset while still maintaining their physical game.

An athlete may begin to feel anxious or develop anxiety about jumping up to the next level in their sport too soon. Coaches and parents often forget to look at a junior elite's maturity level when deciding to jump them up the age bracket or from junior level to senior varsity level.

When it was time for my son to begin playing football in high school, we had to make a tough decision. Because of Bouldin's birth date, he was younger than most of his peers and teammates. In addition to being younger, he was also bigger than the average kid in his class. So naturally, since he had been playing football since first grade, he and everyone else assumed that he would automatically play during his first year in high school.

I knew that Bouldin could ultimately handle playing in ninth grade, but I also knew that his muscle strength needed to catch up to his height, and that his maturity level needed to catch up to the older teammates. This was a decision we both made, and at the end of the day, it was the right one. Not only did he have time to enjoy playing another sport, he was able to develop more than enough strength for the following year in football.

Another explanation could be that the athlete's skills and achievements are so vast that their parents feel that further resources are warranted. They usually assume that by adding more instruction to the athlete's days or adding extra tournaments to their schedule, the athlete might gain an advantage over their peers.

At a younger age, the athlete needs outside interests that have nothing to do with their sport. Their minds cannot handle the constant pressure and demands at such a young age. Their brains need time to develop and learn to balance their current demands before building the momentum that is needed to go to the next level. Most of the time when parents and coaches expect too much out of a young competitor, the athlete will grow to resent the very sport that they once loved.

On the flip side, if the athlete has a solid mindset yet isn't seeing the improvement in their physical game, they may begin to lose interest or feel resentment while observing their peers' faster development.

Each week a player should set small goals for themselves. An athlete needs to see improvement in their performance with the skill that is being taught or practiced each week. By having the athlete set small goals, they will be better able to hold themselves accountable for their own improvement.

If a coach or parent is determining the goals without the input of the athlete, the player will not feel any personal motivation to get the task done. The young mind might even feel resentment toward the added work and begin to push back against the one who is putting the added pressure onto them.

By setting their own goals with the help of their coach each week, the player will feel empowerment in their own physical improvement. Everyone knows that the sense of accomplishment is so much sweeter when we decide for ourselves what needs to be done, then hold ourselves accountable and see it come to fruition.

A Reason Bigger Than Yourself

On the days when the pain feels too much to bear or the times when the pressure seems more than you can handle, there needs to be a greater motivation. You need a significant reason to put your mind and body through the extremes other than the reasons that affect your life right now.

It is difficult to see past the days when you feel defeated and all of your physical and mental energy is drained. *Every athlete has moments in their career when they feel their peers are taking a step forward while they are taking two steps backward in their progress.*

It is on these days that an athlete needs to hold on and remember the big picture. The majority of great pro athletes that withstand the test of time will state a reason why they never gave up. They all have a motivation that was bigger than the roadblocks they faced through their careers.

If you are a young athlete and want to realize a greater purpose for never giving up and pressing through all the challenging workouts that you do every day, take the time to imagine what your ultimate success can do for others. It could be that you want to be a leader and a role model one day for struggling young athletes. Or your motivation could be that you want to be there for your parents, who believed in you and gave up their time and money to see you progress in life.

A common motivator for many aspiring collegiate athletes is to receive a scholarship or a degree that will give them the best education for the future profession they are passionate about.

Whatever your higher motivation is, keep it in the forefront of your mind when times get hard and your mental and physical game seems to be stuck. It will pull you through every time.

CHAPTER 6

Competition—How to Stop Competing Against Yourself

In the end, it's extra effort that separates a winner from second place. But winning takes a lot more than that too. It starts with complete command of the fundamentals. Then it takes desire, determination, discipline, and self-sacrifice. And finally, it takes a great deal of love, fairness, and respect for your fellowman. Put all these together, and even if you don't win, how can you lose.

—Jesse Owens

How much time do you devote to the mental preparation for competition? If you are like many athletes, your mental game takes a backseat to your physical game when it comes time to compete. It is usually when a reoccurring problem arises that a player will seek to undo the damage that has been done to their mindset.

In every other aspect of your sport, you do the work and then see the results. You don't wait until you get injured before you start physically training. So why wait until you are mentally freezing or having meltdowns before you start mentally training concurrently alongside your physical game to have optimal results?

This does not mean to train both your physical and mental game together for only your competition days. Your mental attitude should never vary from one day to the next. This is the very reason so many players have a hard time with their consistency going from their practices to their game days—their mental game is not consistent.

It is only when you decide that every time you put your sports gear on, you will train like you compete with intent, and focus on remaining the same—no matter what is on the agenda for the day. In achieving this, your confident mind will never know the difference between practices and competitions.

StillPoint Insight #8

Mental training and emotional intelligence are aspects that most athletes tend to forget until they are under the pressure to perform.

So, let's begin your mental training for competing. Why do you love the days when it's time to lace up and go toe to toe with an opponent?

Is it the energy of the crowd that is cheering you on? Is it the buzz of adrenaline racing through your system because game day has finally arrived and you know that the excitement from the camaraderie will carry you through? Or do you love competing because you get a chance to prove to yourself and everyone watching that your hard work has paid off?

Depending on the level of experience you have as an athlete, one of these—if not all—would likely be your response. However, there are many players who love every aspect of the game *except* the thought of competing on game day.

I would like to help you change that limited mindset into one that looks forward to the days that you get to prove yourself worthy of your sport.

There are two typical responses I receive when I ask a client why they feel mental resistance while competing. One is the internal pressure they subject themselves to for the need of accomplishment or success. Athletes generally become attached to an expected result or outcome. The mental weight of an expectation alone is enough to weigh an athlete down. You might as well strap ten-pound anklets to your feet.

You will never be able to stay in the present moment and consciously watch or feel what is happening right in front of you if you are thinking about the outcome. And any mishaps that deter you from your expectation will leave you feeling defeated as if the game was already over. There will never be a time in your athletic career when you will know with 100 percent absolute certainty what chain of events will happen, so stop trying.

The only form of certainty that you should have for yourself is the certainty of knowing that by staying in the present moment and focusing on the task in front of you, will you have the strength and endurance to do what your body has been trained to do.

The second answer I normally receive concerns the substantial pressure athletes feel from the external expectations of coaches, parents, and peers. This makes them feel as if a heavy weight is on their chest. The client had lost sight of why or what they wanted for themselves while playing. What has caused the athlete to lose their way is that it has become more about needing to win for someone or something else other than their love for the sport.

If this is an issue you are having, please reread Chapter 5 (Finding Your Intrinsic and Extrinsic Motivation).

StillPoint Insight #9

You will never reach your full potential if you are being pushed by someone other than yourself to succeed.

One concern I've heard when the subject of competition has come up is that rivalry is generally seen as unhealthy, and not aligned with what society believes we should do. A few clients have reluctantly admitted this apprehension to me. They love every aspect of their sport—playing, the camaraderie, and even the demanding physical workouts—but they have a hard time having the killer instinct they need to take an opponent down.

As social awareness has grown, so too has the mindset that you don't need to compete with one another or challenge someone to rise to the top. With that being said, extra rewards and trophies are being given to young children more than ever before.

I remember when my son was given an award at the end of his summer camp for being the best water polo player. The camp counselors had put together a youth camp version of water polo at the beginning of summer. And not wanting to leave any young camper without an award to take home to validate their greatness, Bouldin was deemed the best at something he barely remembered playing.

As Bouldin walked over to me with his medal in hand, he had a slightly confused look upon his face. He proceeded to drop it in my lap and said, "I guess everybody is getting something for nothing."

I understand that most parents have an opinion on this topic and I respect both sides of this heated discussion. However, I believe if competition was taught and looked at differently, I feel fewer rewards would be handed out, but more self-esteem would be gained. The reward of self-confidence that is gained is more than enough for any child growing up and learning what they are capable of accomplishing.

Competition has been perceived as an environment to show dominance over others, thereby allowing an athlete to gain self-worth. In many cases, especially in the junior athletic stage of performance, this is correct. Many athletes will hide their self-doubt and not feel as if they can admit their insecurities to peers, parents, and coaches.

If the reason behind an athlete wanting to play a sport is to prove something or gain attention, they will inevitably take every missed shot personally. Or they may take a game or tournament loss as a direct failure on their part rather than seeing the loss as an opportunity to improve.

Some athletes have forgotten why they love playing their sport or are reluctant to play because of external pressures to the point of admitting they don't want to play the sport at all. When this is combined with intentions of proving self-worth, anxiety can become a factor.

These young athletes might demonstrate heightened emotions, tantrums, or exaggerated pessimistic statements—or even signs of singling out others to intimidate. These characteristics are not just found in the sporting world; they can be observed in anyone—at any age—who does not believe in themselves or in why they are doing something to begin with. Many of these individuals feel the need to prove themselves worthy in others' eyes.

When intimidation or harassment of others becomes a factor, the aggressor may prey on teammates they perceive as weaker, mentally or physically. More times than not, the player is currently or has previously experienced verbal intimidation themselves in their own life. So bullying can rear its ugly head because the previous victim feels the need to gain their own confidence back by dominating another.

Tantrums usually arise when a player is of the opinion that they are not getting their way with calls by the game officials. Or an outburst may surface when an athlete is not playing up to their ability because of a mental disruption. They may then begin to act as if their ability was physically taken away from them by a higher power and they now are unable to perform.

Instead of looking within and seeing the mistakes they made, they will lash out and blame others. We have all seen this play out, even with professional players on television.

Exaggerated pessimistic statements can be heard while the player is performing. "It's not fair! They were cheating," they might say. Or the pessimistic emotions will be carried over after the loss, with long periods of isolation and/or sulking. The overall theme? "It never works out for me. They had an unfair advantage."

If the reason behind an athlete's physical performance is they are using their sport to try to find self-worth or attempting to prove something to someone else, the athlete is setting themselves up for mental failure, which will be realized in their resulting score. Not only will the competitor not go the distance, but they will always be striving for approval in other areas of their life.

If this sounds a little too close to home for you, then stop and take the time to reevaluate your reasons for playing. Your only priority is yourself and your own happiness. The individuals that you feel the need to prove something to are not putting in the blood, sweat, and tears that you are.

Begin to understand that you are proving something to yourself every day just by competing. You are growing in awareness of your abilities and intellect every time you gear up to play.

You'll be like the pitcher who is continually honing their arsenal, making adjustments to their approach, and learning the tendencies of the opposition in order to maintain dominance.

Look inside yourself and find the reasons why you want to personally put in the effort to succeed. Only then will you find the balance and exhilaration you once had playing your sport, while also finding mental clarity and balance in your life.

Looking at Competition Differently

If you want to take your game to the next level, you may find an advantage by perceiving competition differently. Instead of looking at competition as competing against opponents, view it as competing against yourself. Discover value in finding motivation to challenge yourself to see what you are really capable of.

It is human nature to want to excel over another while going one step further in achieving something that we have set out to do for ourselves. If there were no mental or physical opposition to keep us on our toes, we would probably not take that extra step. If there were no obstacles or challenges, a competitor may not even bother committing their time and sweat to the extreme workouts and practices that they need to take on. Discovering what your mind and body is capable of is a reward that cannot be denied or one that can be taken away.

Building your cognizance is the true payoff. Since the moment you began having your own conscious thoughts versus your parents' beliefs, your mind and body's only prerogative was to learn and grow from one moment to the next. I am imagining that anything that has ever held your interest for more than five minutes is something you wanted to learn more about. I'm willing to bet that the first time you watched or played your sport, something clicked; it just felt right to you. It was that initial interest or excitement that caused you to want more.

It is only after internal or external expectations are placed upon you that the initial attraction you once had from the sport gets diminished. Instead of thinking *I want to, I cannot wait to,* you begin thinking *I should, I have to, or I need to.*

If you can view your sport with the child-like enthusiasm and curiosity that you once had, then you will view your opponent only as an obstacle to scale over and not as a potential threat that will smash your ego into a wall.

Look forward to the competition and the hurdles that are in front of you. If deep down you did not truly enjoy the challenges, or if you did not have these oppositions staring you in the face, you probably would not want to be there in the first place.

Here is a perfect example from one of my clients that will help explain this concept about obstacles being something you actually want.

A professional golfer, she repeatedly stated that she dreaded sand traps, almost to the point of anxiousness when she had faced them. (For all the non-golfers reading this, a sand trap is exactly as it sounds—it is a large pile of depressed sand in various places on the golf course. If a ball is hit into a sand trap, it can be challenging to lob the ball out and have a good placement for your next shot.)

Her resistance to sand traps caused her to perceive them as a hindrance in her game. I remember asking her how much she would enjoy the game if the sand traps were nonexistent. She immediately exclaimed that she would love it. I asked her to take thirty seconds and just imagine what the golf course would look and play like if there were no sand traps.

I asked her to visualize a golf course where there were no sand traps or water hazards to be seen. Then I added, while you're at it, take the trees out of the equation as well. At this point, she started to catch on to what I was suggesting to her. If there were no obstacles on the golf course, what fun would it be to play? Within three holes, even kids would be bored out of their minds playing miniature golf if there was nothing to maneuver around or go inside to entice them.

After that day—armed with a new mindset toward sand traps and an eagerness to take them on if needed—she began losing the anxiousness that she had once felt. My client even recalled that as a junior elite she had always loved and looked forward to the challenges. She realized that it was those very same challenges that kept her focused and driven back then.

The point is, wouldn't you find it boring playing your sport if no one ever passed you, struck you out, tackled you, or ever mentally challenged you? Yes, you would have already found something else to do with your time and energy to stimulate your mind.

The bottom line is there will always be aspects of your sport that do not cause you to jump out of bed with excitement, but if you remember that wanting to be bored and stagnant within your sport was not the reason you started playing, you will view the perceived hurdles very differently. And while you're at it, remember that learning to overcome any obstacle or facing a difficult situation will only build your confidence.

If more confidence is what you need, in the following chapter I will go over the underlying reasons players begin to lose confidence in their sport and how to regain the needed self-assurance.

CHAPTER 7

Confidence in Yourself and in Your Ability to Perform

Circumstance does not make the man, it reveals him to himself.

—James Allen

How can you ever know what it means to have confidence within yourself if you have never voluntarily or involuntarily been in a challenging situation where you desperately needed self-reliance?

On the day you were born into the world, the gift of confidence was not handed to you on a silver platter. In fact, as a newborn you were screaming your tiny little head off because you had just emerged into a world that was unknown to you.

From that moment on, every experience you had to face was new, even if quite often you were hiding behind your mother's leg. As the years began to pass and you gained more confidence with each new experience you tackled, your self-assurance was gaining momentum in most areas of your life. However, doubt and uncertainty also began to show their ugly heads.

Parents, teachers, and coaches are often quick to point out perceived limitations in children, not understanding the internal damage they are doing to the kids. And if the limitations are being built upon with continued affirmations as opposed to being worked on and altered, the children will eventually believe these things about themselves.

Confidence is not something you are born with. It is gained by living through experiences in which you are challenged by what you believe are your weaknesses—the areas in your life in which you imagine that you are vulnerable and less sure of yourself.

The perceived weak spot that I needed to overcome was my belief in myself as a writer. For years, while working one on one with clients, I filled notebooks with research, notes, and ideas on what I knew would help the individuals that I did not have the pleasure to work with. However, it froze me in my tracks knowing that someone was going to be reading the words that had been hand-written on legal pads and turned into some form of typed document.

It has taken me several years to finally gain my courage to write what I do truly believe will assist many athletes for years to come.

Who you are or what you may do professionally has no bearing on the topic of confidence—everyone has an area in their life in which they lack self-esteem. This is the area in your life in which you always second-guess the decisions you make or overanalyze every possible scenario that could play out from your decision.

For example, a client that I worked with was confident in her physical ability and often measurably out-performed everyone on the team. Yet she was ostracized by her teammates off the court because she came across as being shy and reluctant to engage with any of them.

Ever since she was a young girl, she had been told by her parents and relatives that other than when she was playing her sport, she always seemed to carry herself timidly and was socially awkward in public.

Unless she was speaking to girls about sporting events or the team's experiences—topics she was comfortable discussing—anxiety would rise up and she would begin to no longer hear what was being said over the sound of the blood pounding in her skull. And the result always led to feelings of embarrassment, as well as discomfort coming from her teammates as they watched her humiliated reaction.

She had always believed that she was an introvert by nature. Since the time she was little, she was repeatedly told that she was shy and needed to be more confident in herself.

After working with her a while, I found that in fact she did not have an introverted personality. She was actually outgoing in a one-on-one setting. She also had quite a funny sense of humor—she had just kept it to herself all of these years because of her the lack of self-confidence.

My client had never really had an opportunity to learn how to be around many kids at once. Her parents were strict with her upbringing and had decided that homeschooling would benefit her more than attending public school.

For as long as she could remember, if she was not working on her schoolwork, she was training for her sport in one form or another. In all my client's younger years, she never had the chance to learn how to adapt and socialize like the other girls her age.

If you feel as if you lack confidence because of a personality trait you believe you may have, ask yourself:

- What is the evidence for and against this belief?
- On what grounds are you basing this assumption?
- Are you considering all the external factors that might be attributing to this belief and clouding your judgment?

How can you let go of what you thought was a belief about yourself? Break it down and see where it might have originated. What were the circumstances that were surrounding this notion?

Once you gain insight with self-truth (and with forgiveness toward those who might have played a role in planting this seed of belief into your mind), you can begin to clear it and finally let go of the past. In this moment, your point of power is *now, in this moment*, to decide how you want to distinguish yourself and how you want to live your life.

However, unlike the client I described above, most athletes do have confidence in their personal lives. It is in their game where the lack of confidence usually comes into play and ultimately messes with their mindset. Generally, players will begin to have uncertainty for several different reasons, which I've outlined in detail below.

No. 1: The fear of failure

The fear of failure will have you playing defensively with the intention of not losing as opposed to playing with the mindset to win. This fear will cause you to tighten up, hold your breath, and play protectively instead of playing as you should—with your strengths and with the pure intent of winning.

Every athlete faces losses in their career, but when their fear of failure overrides their determination to win, the loss is felt much more deeply because they know that it was their lack of self-confidence that caused them to not perform to their full potential. Fear of failure can come from several sources, including:

- fear of letting your parents or coaches down after they have given so much of their time toward your dream and investing in your potential;
- fear of letting yourself down;
- fear of losing the lead that you have gained in your tournament or game;
- fear stemming from a consistency of recent matches lost;
- fear of losing to your peers and feeling embarrassment or resentment.

Fear of failure is an emotional threat, but one that can be turned into an emotional advantage. Instead of letting this fear make you feel helpless and wanting to avoid the threat, turn it into an emotional challenge.

Any emotion can be used as an advantage, even the emotion of anger if caught quick enough. Anger can cause you to increase your intensity and sharpen your focus. It can also propel you to want to fight harder and strengthen your resolve not to give up.

Whenever you catch yourself feeling fear, shift the heightened emotion into a sudden burst of anger for feeling doubt within yourself, and use it to drive your focus to compete relentlessly for what you want and what you deserve.

The baseball player who was recently beaned is understandably skittish stepping back into the batter's box, but they need to channel that apprehension into an emotion that will drive them forward to regain their focus as a hitter.

As Nelson Mandela said, "I learned that courage was not the absence of fear, but the triumph over it. The brave man is not he who does not feel afraid, but he who conquers that fear."

You should also realize that fear and excitement can cause the same physical reactions within your body. When you find yourself having an emotional reaction, take a moment to check in to see if you are anxious about *wanting* to go out to prove to yourself what you are capable of, or if you feel anxious about *having* to go out to prove to others what you're capable of doing.

If you can change your perception to one of anticipating the challenge—to only proving to yourself what your capabilities are—you can use your body's reaction to your benefit.

If you cannot seem to let go of the fear, identify what is causing you to feel afraid and confront it with self-truth along with self-forgiveness. Everyone has moments of fear of failing. If you were never afraid of losing in your sport, it would indicate to me that you were not as passionate about playing as you should be.

No. 2: Lack of self-confidence in their ability

There are two areas in an athlete's sport in which a player needs to have confidence. A player needs absolute confidence while performing in practice and extreme self-confidence while competing. We will separate the two by calling them *performance self-confidence* and *competitive self-confidence*.

Performance self-confidence for an athlete refers to the confidence they have for themselves before, after, and especially during practices and workouts. Performance self-confidence is a player's self-assurance. They know they have held themselves accountable for all they were mentally and physically capable of doing for their training.

Competitive self-confidence signifies an athlete's confidence that they can take the same ability that they performed in practice into games when they feel the pressure to perform at their best.

Commonly, athletes will have self-confidence in their performance before games, but will not have the certainty of themselves to perform under pressure when the competition begins, and something is on the line.

If an athlete only feels confident in their practice game and thinks their lack of confidence from past competitions has held them back, they will start to either overanalyze the game before it even begins or play the early stages of the game defensively until their nerves settle down.

Believe it or not, there are players who rely heavily on their competitive self-confidence and neglect the performance training that is needed to take them to the next level. The lack of confidence in knowing they have not held themselves accountable either out of laziness or ego causes the player to settle in their current level or rankings. They do not have the belief in their ability to level up.

If any of these reasons resonate with you, try the following:

- Recognize that the lack of confidence you are feeling in your competition performance is a common occurrence that many athletes have faced in their careers. Once you accept that this is a universal attribute among many athletes at all levels, you can move past the self-judgment and begin to find ways of overcoming this hurdle.
- Be patient, as gaining self-confidence takes time to form. Learn to give yourself positive feedback and begin to acknowledge all the amazing things you accomplish throughout each day while playing your sport and in your personal life.
- Always remember to let the punishment fit the crime. If you make a mistake, do not blow it out of proportion. Extremely negative emotional reactions to the slightest of errors will cause an athlete to become worked up and they will begin to lose focus on what their strategy is for the next play. High-level athletes know how to be objective about their mistakes and not over-identify with an emotion that does not fit the crime.
- Before going into a competitive game, take the time to align yourself and visualize the type of player that you want recognized as by the players around you.
- Notice when another player is displaying confidence in their game. Begin to mirror and emulate that energy for your own benefit.

- Always give yourself a fist pump or a mental high-five when you do something great. Your brain will reward you with a great chemical release that will energize you, with an added benefit of imprinting what you did to memory.

- Know that in every game or tournament in which you compete, you will either *win* or *learn*. You can never really lose a game if there is something that was gained from it. Never give yourself excuses of why you did not win. Take a moment and have self-truth regarding what mistakes you made, then make a mental note to work on them the following week. But most importantly, get over the self-pity and move on to concentrate on your next game.

No. 3: Overanalyzing their mechanics while competing

If you have an analytical personality, you may tend to overanalyze your mechanics while competing. This may may cause you to be overly critical of yourself when the pressure is on. Depending on your sport, it is impossible for you to concentrate on what is playing out in front of you if you are scrutinizing your technique every chance you get.

Overanalyzing may also cause you to spend valuable time evaluating your opponent's game, and this will cause distractions in your own. When an athlete is rigid in their analytical thinking process, they can easily become emotional to the point of becoming extremely agitated when they feel that they are not performing exactly as they should be. Striving to be a perfectionist should only be done in practices or lessons, otherwise it will become a distraction during gameplay when it matters most.

Here's how to overcome this dynamic:

- Define your goals and objectives each day but also allow for creative thinking to have its place in your game.
- Set the intention to only focus on one or two techniques during your lessons so that you can practice quieting the mind to let your natural instincts kick in. Basically, relax your thinking brain and let your body perform as it has been trained to do.
- When you are learning a new technique at a lesson or practice, notice when you're feeling frustrated or overwhelmed. Take a step back to reset. Feel your chest rising and falling with each breath you take. Give yourself a moment to remember why you love the sport you're playing. Then, when you feel yourself settling down, set an intention of remaining calm and staying focused in the moment. Just as you have absorbed every other technique in the past, this is just another one to ingest.
- If you find yourself not being able to change this pattern while competing, focus on your execution of the fundamentals rather than fishing for technical changes.

No. 4: Not being aware of their body language during competitions

A big part of competition is about body language and nonverbal communication. Competitors have to stake their claim by demonstrating through body language that they are eager to take on whatever the opponent brings to the table. This is important because it illustrates to you and your adversary where your head is at.

If your shoulders are slumped and your eyes are looking at the ground while you're not actively playing, it reflects that you lack confidence. Additionally, if you exhibit negative self-talk loud enough for your opponent and everyone else within earshot to hear, it indicates to the opponent that you are in a noncoherent mindset and they can now take advantage of this. Your opponent will either repeat the action to bring about the same extravagated response or they'll know they now have the opportunity to go on the offensive while you are in this tantrum mode.

StillPoint Insight #10

Focus only on the perception you want to convey to the world, not on what you feel the world's perception is of you.

Here are some techniques to overcome this:

- If you make an error, do a physical shadow movement of the correct movement. Not only will this mentally reestablish what is to be done correctly next time, but it will also let your opponent know that your head is still in the game as opposed to being distracted by your last error.
- Make sure to always look your opponent in the eye while speaking with them and use a clear strong voice to convey what it is that you are saying. This sends a strong signal that you are ready to take on any challenge that comes your way.

- While walking to your assigned position on the playing field, draw your shoulders back and stand tall at your full height. This will release an extra boost of testosterone into your system, which will only increase the self-confidence that you need.

No. 5: Getting stuck in training mode

If you are an athlete who practices all week and spends all your time taking lessons to work on your technical skills rather than playing games where you are being held accountable, you can get stuck in training mode. This can cause you to concentrate too heavily on your technical skills as opposed to just playing your game. You will also be unprepared for the pressure you will feel when you are up against a real opponent, who will not give you leeway when you make errors as your coach may.

Here's how you can overcome this challenge:

- When you're playing a match or game where there is something on the line, learn to let go of the instructional components and become present in the moment, so you can focus on getting the job done that you already know instinctively how to do.
- Spend an equal amount of time participating in practice matches so that when it comes time to play matches that count, you will be better able to handle the mental pressure.
- Use the coach's and your own time wisely. When taking a lesson, go with the intent of zeroing in on what the coach is instructing. Practice the directives repetitively until

they become a habit, so that you will not need numerous lessons to perfect the techniques later.

- During practice matches, only concentrate on one or two goals so that you can still focus on learning the new concepts your coach is bringing to your game while at the same time freeing your mind to focus on winning the match.

We all have occasional doubts about our ability to rise to the challenge, but confidence will only come to you if you face each and every obstacle head-on, no matter what the outcome is. Because the fact of the matter is, you showed up to the game!

CHAPTER 8

Do Your Habits Reflect Your Goals?

Excellence is not a singular act but a habit. You are what you do repeatedly.

-Shaquille O'Neal

Do you know that roughly 40 percent of the daily actions that you perform are habits that you have acquired?

What was the first thing you did this morning when your alarm went off? Maybe it was to check your phone, like most people do. Was it to jump straight out of bed and into the shower? Or maybe it was to lie in bed and begin to dread the day that is before you. Whichever it may be, the habits you have when you first get up in the morning have been formed over a long time.

These mundane habits may not seem important to you, but many of your other habits directly reflect on the goals that you have for yourself.

Having goals is fundamental if you are an athlete. Many of you reading this book are already aware of this fact. Having goals allows you to focus on what's needed for your performance now and in the future.

Without setting goals for yourself, what is there to keep you going as you improve yourself? If you are an athlete, you will never get to the next level without mentally and physically evolving.

Most young adults have long-term goals they have set for themselves. But, without having short- and mid-term goals, too, the long-term goals will feel a million miles away. When you are training to run in a marathon, it takes many short- and mid-length distance runs to prepare you before your goal is possible.

Short-Term Goals

Short-term goals are the objectives that you can start working on now. Below are a few examples of short-term goals:

- making the decision to not miss one practice or workout unless it is due to an injury;
- beginning to increase your workouts by 10 to 15 percent;
- deciding from this point on that you will take your practices and workouts just as seriously as you do your games and tournaments;
- choosing wisely who you will associate with—making the conscious decision that your network of friends will only be motivating and like-minded in their goals;

- resolving yourself to decrease your social media time by 20 percent each day or more depending on the amount of "drifting" time you spend now staring at your phone;
- selecting a more beneficial diet for your body type and sport.

By setting short-terms goals, you will be holding yourself accountable, which in turn will increase your self-confidence. As we covered last chapter, having confidence in yourself is one of the most important things you can have as a competitor.

Accomplishing your short-term goals has the added benefit of helping you to see that every setback that may come across is not the end of world or the death of your athletic career.

Mid-Term Goals

Many books and coaches will advise you to have short-term and long-term goals. While this is great advice, I feel there is another area that is not covered enough: mid-term goals.

You should decide what areas in your life you can change now, meaning in the short term. Also opt to have mid-term goals—ambitions you have chosen that are achievable within six months to a year. Here are some examples of mid-term goals:

- increasing your overall speed;
- achieving a jump in rankings;
- gaining or dropping the appropriate weight for your sport;
- setting your sights on raising your grade point average if you are a collegiate or high school athlete;
- increasing your physical endurance while building up your mental resilience.

Mid-term goals allow you to adjust your future or long-term goal to one that is more realistic for you if you need to. I am not writing this to diminish any dreams that you may have. On the contrary, I am suggesting that by being realistic in your future goals based upon your athletic ability, you can modify your future objective to one that is attainable and will be more rewarding for you in the long run. By staying in athletics with self-awareness of your capabilities, you will achieve higher success than the life you would have without continuing in athletics.

Once they believe or have been told that they do not have what it takes to play at a D1 level or the potential to go professional in their sport, many athletes in high school will give up or not put in as much hard work. Even if your athletic abilities do not seem strong enough to take you to a D1 school, there are many great schools for you to strive for.

I hear such regret in the voices of the individuals who gave up entirely or who did not keep up with the rigorous pace still needed to play in a D2 or D3 college. These colleges not only give scholarships but also may be the perfect fit for a successful career.

Think of your short-term goals as stepping-stones that will put you onto the right path. Your mid-term goals, meanwhile, are your strategic pathway. Finally, your long-term goals will lead you down the precise road toward your success in whatever it is that you want to become or accomplish.

As I mentioned in the beginning of the chapter, most athletes are aware of their long-term desires and are possibly already striving to accomplish their short-term goals. However, if they are not aware of their daily habits, players will be delayed—if not shoved off—those stepping-stones every time.

What are the daily habits you repeat unconsciously? Here are a few examples of bad habits that need to be broken:

- falling asleep later than the time you had set for yourself because you were mindlessly drifting through social media before going to bed;
- skipping breakfast in the morning because you are repeatedly running late to get out the door, or you've gotten into the habit of not eating breakfast at all;
- drinking caffeine throughout the day instead of drinking enough water for hydration and recovery;
- leaving your disgusting used gear by the door when you come in from practice instead of changing it out so you're ready to walk out the door the next day on time;
- goofing off and socializing during the first twenty minutes of practice before starting to take the day's training seriously.

All of these bad habits and many others negatively affect your ability to carry out your goals. By establishing healthy habits, you can accomplish your goals and build self-confidence in your ability to hold yourself accountable.

If you were to look at most professional athletes and what their daily routine habits are, you would see why they have achieved the level of success they have. If your long-term goal or dream is to become a professional athlete, why would you not decide here and now to clean up your less-than-stellar tendencies and start practicing the beneficial habits the skilled professionals have?

StillPoint Insight #11

Believe it or not, healthy habits are just as easy to
form as the ones that have a negative impact.

Most of your habitual routines are formed unconsciously. The mundane routines like brushing your top teeth first before the bottom teeth or tying your right shoe as opposed to the left first. Or the order in which you get dressed in the morning. All allow your mind to focus on more important matters as you leave your house for the day. Imagine if you did not have routine habits. You would have to consciously think about how to brush your teeth, or physically watch yourself tie your shoestrings. These routines are stored in your brain to help your mind work more efficiently.

However, some negative conscious habits are formed out of laziness. For instance, waiting to do your homework or chores until the last minute, or not taking the time the day before you leave to make sure you have everything you need for the weekend tournament. A very common harmful habit for a lot of athletes is to skip stretching or setting aside a pre-warmup routine before a game.

Habits are formed because there is always an award attached to the routine. How about looking at the rewards you receive for the proactive habits?

There is the obvious incentive of achieving your life-long dream. But how about some of the other rewards you get from setting new habits? These include:

- feeling a sense of accomplishment;
- seeing improvement in your performance;

- dealing with less aggravation from your parents and coaches;
- having more self-confidence when you look in the mirror;
- coming up with more time and energy to do the things you enjoy doing outside of your sport;
- gaining the maturity and independence needed to become an elite athlete.

These are just a few examples of what you can get by setting and following through with improved habits. In addition, you can also consciously reward yourself with indulgences that, if needed, will give you a little push to help establish and set into motion theses new routines.

If you want to break the bad habit of drinking too much caffeine, one allowance could be granting yourself something caffeinated every other day. If you decide to hold yourself more accountable with your social media time, then a compromise in the form of a reward could be setting a limit of thirty minutes of mindless drifting after everything is checked off your list for the day. (Of course, make sure that it does not interfere with the time you set for yourself to go to sleep!)

The incentive I like to suggest for my clients is to designate days, at least twice a month, when you allow yourself to have no responsibilities. Of course, let people in your life who need to know it that this is your day to see or do anything that you want.

You may feel as if you already have relaxed routines or habits that work for you. And even if they're not as structured as you know they should be, you feel as if they are working well enough for you. Let me assure you, when you are putting off something that needs to be done now—and using that time to goof off—you are not enjoying it as much as you think you are. In the back of your mind there is judgment, whether it is self-judgment or the certainty that it will come from your frustrated parents or coaches. Any form of judgment will only weigh down the feeling of freedom you believe that you are experiencing.

I would like to introduce something that will greatly help you in forming new habits while accomplishing everything else more efficiently. I call the concept "time segments." But first, I'll give you a little more information on how the brain works for and against you.

The human brain has three main parts. The first part is primitive and is known as the instinctual brain. This section of the brain goes off your instinct and works with your basic bodily functions. The instinctual brain is meant to keep you alive by staying in touch with your essential human needs such as hunger and thirst. Your heart rate and reproductive drive are also driven by your instinctual (survival) brain.

The second part of the brain is the emotional brain. This part of the mind is involved with your emotions. The emotional brain is where your feelings of joy, sadness, or anger originate. This component is significant because based on the level of emotions that are attached to a memory, the brain will store away this knowledge for further use.

Let me elaborate. Have you ever played at a location where you had a terrible loss as an athlete? You may have found yourself saying *I hate playing here, I have never played well at this location.* Well, your emotional brain is responsible for this attachment to the memory based on your emotional response associated with this place.

The third brain is our conscious brain, otherwise known as the cortex. Our conscious brain forms opinions based on your first and second (instinctual and emotional) brains, meaning your instincts and emotions can help you to consider the consequences of an action and help to make a deliberate decision on how to proceed in any given situation.

An annoying aspect of the conscious brain is that it does not work on autopilot. When your emotional brain is in overdrive, your conscious brain will take a back seat and enjoy watching your emotional outburst over missing your putt or losing three games in a row in tennis to a less talented player. It is only when you become consciously aware of your speeding emotions before they get out of hand that you're allowed to place the conscious brain back into the driver's seat.

Throughout our day, we are using the first, second, and third part of our brain at any given time. Depending on the interest and character traits of the individual, one or two parts will be operational depending on what task is in front of them. Many people will react mostly out of instinct alone with no thought to the consequences they may face. Doing so allows the emotional brain freedom to react to the aftermath of the instinctual impulse.

For an athlete, the instinctual, emotional, and conscious brains need to be fired up to achieve optimal performance. If you have been playing your sport for some time, then you want your instincts to play a part in your game. Your emotional brain is vital in fueling and driving you to perform at your best. If you were not emotional about your sport, you would not be passionate about it. But when you harness your emotions, you can steer them into focused energy and drive for the mental endurance that is needed to compete at your best.

Only by having your conscious brain in the driver's seat and staying focused in the present moment will you be able to consider the consequences and make a deliberate decision about what action needs to take place.

An athlete does at least ten to twenty more hours of extra work each week than their nonathletic peers. As a result, they have many more additional preoccupations going on in their heads. This makes it extremely difficult to focus on what they need or want to do throughout the day or while playing their sport.

When I begin working with a client, early on I strongly encourage that they start implementing time segments into their life.

StillPoint Insight #12

If you are in a thick, heavy mindset filled with clutter clouding your vision, then your outer reality will reflect the mess you have going on inside your mind.

Time Segments

The practice of using time segments is not only great for forming new habits, it is also useful for keeping your thoughts present in the moment. Time segments are about setting an intention for what you want to accomplish within a short period of time. Time segments are exactly what they sound like. You break down your day into individual time slots, starting when you wake in the morning until the moment you shut your eyes at night. Literally before your head even lifts off the pillow and you open your eyes, until the moment you walk out the door to leave for the day, decide for that segment how you want to feel. Do you want to feel motivated and energized because you will be playing your sport that morning? Do you want to feel focused or determined for a meeting or test that you will be facing? Do you want to feel calm and be collected for something that you are anxious about facing?

Once you are aware of the intention you need to set for yourself, you can then decide the thoughts and actions that will put you into that mindset. Is it motivating music that would put you into the right headspace? Is it a great breakfast, so that you will not be distracted by hunger? Once you have decided on your best course of action, do not deter from it. Do not allow distractions or wayward thoughts to get in your way.

An important reason that it is smart to break the day into individual sections is that it's much easier to stay focused with your thoughts and intentions for short periods of time as opposed to allowing your thoughts about your day's agenda to overlap with one another.

As soon as you walk out the door in the morning, determine the outcome you want to have happen for the first segment once you get to your destination. The result you want to achieve may be to make a great impression on someone. Or if you have been neglectful recently and found that you have not given 100 percent of your mind and body in the classroom or in your sport, then this would be the perfect time to set that goal for yourself.

Time segments are not about only setting an intention for how you want to portray yourself going into an experience, it is also about determining the outcome you want to achieve by the end of that segment.

The visual that I like to give to my clients depicting how most individuals experience their day is that of a pinball machine. Imagine that you are the ball. You are being pulled back by the lever, virtually being launched out, which marks the beginning of your day.

The first object that you hit, meaning the direction of your thoughts that you may have, ricochets you out of alignment. Perhaps they are negative recollections about something that happened the night before, or dreading your schedule for the day ahead.

The second factor that may ping you out of having a great start to your day could be a tedious email you read, or perhaps an encounter with someone nagging at you for not doing something that you should have done the day before.

Before you know it, you are halfway through the day and you have had your bell rung numerous times. More than likely, you felt trapped by other people's agendas. You did not get into the right mindset before going into each experience and did not set an intention for how you wanted those individual segments to end.

For example, let's say that you've been frustrated recently because your coach has been rough on you and they do not seem to be letting up anytime soon. As you are on your way to practice, several of their embarrassing verbal assaults are being replayed over and over in your mind. Make the decision that, today, instead of letting a repeat performance play out, this is your opportunity to consciously decide on a different outcome.

Before going into practice, think back. What is the main theme that the coach has been trying to call you out on? Is it that you have not been focusing on practice, that you have been goofing off instead of taking it seriously because you are second or third string? Maybe it's because you don't understand what they want from you. Instead of getting clarification privately, you have been resisting and trying to push your way through it.

Whatever the reason is, before starting your practice is the right time to decide that, today, at the conclusion of this time segment, the result will be vastly different than the previous practices. This is also the best time to decide on a way of going about fixing your previous slip-ups. No matter what happens at training that day, you will know that instead of reacting from your emotions, you took control of a situation that you felt was happening to you.

Going into any time segment with a deliberate intention will have a dramatic effect on your future outcomes, and soon this will become a habit. In fact, you will instantly recognize when you have not yet set clear intentions for yourself, by the evidence of the thoughts you are having and the experiences that are playing out. After a while, you will recognize that you benefit from a proactive mindset because your ego appreciates the results it gets by being more in control of what you want to have happen.

If you practice time segments, you will see that you are more in control of your life experiences than you previously believed. You will also have added efficiency to your time and energy. And since you are an athlete with less free time on your hands than the majority of your peers, time segments will feel like a blessing.

StillPoint Insight #13

If you go about your day with set intentions, whatever
it is that you are intent on accomplishing will seem
as if you were running a 5K versus a marathon.

As a side note, when I had finished writing this chapter on goals and habits, I sent it to a great friend to read. In his email response, he said that his high school coach had given him and his teammates an assignment to write down their goals and read them aloud to one another. I asked him to expand on this experience and how it benefited the team. This is what he said:

> When I was a teenager, "accountability" was something my high school basketball coach taught us. Now, accountability in this particular situation relates to a team sport. It can be related to an individual sport as well, obviously, though in a slightly different form. The exercise was that at the end of the season, our coach would get us together. We would talk openly about what our team goals were for next year. He would then have each of us write them down, and how we would attain them. There were small short-term goals as well as longer-term ones that were pie in the sky, harder-to-achieve goals.
>
> The point was, we wrote them down and shared them as a team with each other. Our coach then put a plan in place on how we were going to

achieve those goals. We were now "accountable" on what we put pen to paper to. By doing this, it brought us closer as a team, a family. We now were pushing each other to "achieve" by holding each other accountable. It was forward-thinking back then, but we all bought in, because we all had great respect for our coach and believed in his vision.

We fortunately were not only very talented physically, but mentally tough as nails as well. This, along with the goal exercise, was the perfect combination. It brought us closer together, as we cared about each other, because we all had skin in the game.

In an individual sport, sitting down with your coach and talking about what your goals are for the upcoming season, then writing them down and discussing what needs to be done to achieve them, was the key. But it is all on you. You have to have the self-motivation, by making yourself accountable, to achieve your goals.

Bottom line is that if you have the shotgun approach, rather than the rifle approach, you're doomed for failure. It's like you hear the saying, practice makes perfect. Well, no. Perfect practice makes perfect. You have to have a plan, goals, and accountability, or you will only have soft results.

By putting the rifle approach into your daily routine with accountability, it doesn't mean they will all be achieved, but it will set you up for success. Without a plan, you're doomed to fail.

CHAPTER 9

How to Become a Clutch Player

When the mind is controlled and spirit aligned with purpose, the body is capable of so much more than we realize.

—Rich Roll

So, you want to become a clutch player. Perhaps you'd like to sink a putt seven feet from the eighteenth hole. Maybe you want to sink a three-pointer with seconds left on the clock or catch an errant pass in the end zone to win the game.

A clutch performance in sports is the ability of athletes under pressure or *in the clutch* in the last minutes of the game to call upon strength and focused intent to perform with elite consciousness. Anyone can come through on occasion in a pivotal situation, but some athletes consistently perform better than others when the stakes are high.

It is easier than ever to become a clutch player now that more awareness is being placed on the mental side of the game. You might feel that some players were born with the *clutch gene*.

However, University of Alabama football Head Coach Nick Saban has a different view:

> We have five choices in our life. We can be bad at what we do. We can be average at what we do. We can be good at what we do, which is God's expectation for whatever ability he gave us. Or we can be excellent or we can be elite.
>
> Everybody has a choice as to what they want to do and how they want to do it. But, if you are going to be excellent or elite, you have to do special things. You have to have special focus. Special commitment, drive, and passion to do things at a higher level, a high standard at all times.
>
> It does not matter what God-given ability that you have, that probably makes you good. But, without the rest of it, I'm not sure you will ever be excellent or elite. And that is the part we're trying to get to.

Many fans still debate whether Tim Tebow was the best clutch quarterback ever in college football. In basketball you may feel that the greatest clutch players include Lebron James and the late Kobe Bryant. But I believe the ultimate clutch athlete in basketball history was Michael Jordan.

Take a look at the shot he made against the Cleveland Cavaliers in the 1989 playoffs or watch his performance in what was coined the Flu Game in the 1997 finals. Even if you only saw him dunking the game-winner the following season, you would agree that Jordan is undoubtedly the most clutch player in basketball history.

But how do you become like Tim and Michael? Emotions, interest, and attention are three components necessary if an athlete wants to compete with the confidence that it takes to maintain their composure when the game is on the line.

You need to have a firm grip on your emotions. In addition, your primary interest, day in and day out, should be on knowing every possible piece of information about the sport and the position you play. You should also have a keen awareness of your opponent.

I believe that scrutinizing an opponent has long been overlooked in team sports in the past. A player should have first-hand knowledge and a good understanding of the players that they are going toe-to-toe with. If they know the signals that the players on the other team typically unconsciously send out, they can take the advantage over the opponent to win the game.

Let's now dive into the third component, which is focused attention on staying present. The player's attention must be held in the present moment. This intent to have situational awareness in the present moment must be placed on every second of the game.

Situational awareness is important to the idea of clutch play. Having situational awareness is critical for making game-winning decisions while under pressure. This means that you must have selective attention, dynamic attention, and sustained attention.

Let me explain what these each mean:

- Selective Attention allows you to filter out distractions and prioritize visual processing.
- Dynamic Attention is the ability to keep on top of things that are moving or changing rapidly.
- Sustained Attention means you are able to maintain attention for an extended period of time.

When a player's focus is on the outcome of the game versus the execution of the play right in front of them, they may choke. Most athletes are aware of and have experienced this crushing blow, but do you know the physical changes that you experience before mentally choking in a game? By knowing the signs, you may be able to get a grip on your attention and pull out a clutch play.

Here are some signs to watch out for:

- Your thought process is less logical and more emotional.
- Your heartrate will increase noticeably.
- You may sweat more than what is normally associated with the activity.
- You may look at your surroundings in a scattered and distracted way.

However, the more obvious sign that you are not playing in a state of flow is when your shots, throws, kicks, or swings are off the mark. If you have been playing your sport for a long time, you no longer need to consciously analyze how you perform while playing in the moment. Your muscle memory will take care of that. But if you are experiencing a stress response to pressure in the game, your muscles will tense up.

When the body is stressed, muscles tense up. This tension in the muscles is a reflexive reaction to stress. Your body is not aware of whether you are in physical danger or having a stress response to a sport that you are playing. Your body is only aware of the signal that your brain has sent it, letting it know that you are in fight or flight mode. The tensing of your muscles is the body's way of guarding against injury or pain.

If your muscles are constricted and you wish to perform a specific motor task that is already in your muscle memory from constant repetition, whatever you do will go awry. That sweet spot to which you normally would have pitched a perfect ball is going to be off by an inch. If the muscles in your arms are constrained, you will not have the flexibility or the arm span that you would usually have.

Elite Consciousness

If you master the art of staying present with intent and focus, you will be able to perform with elite consciousness. You will have the ability to make intuitive decisions quickly based on behavioral patterns happening in front of you. If you are staying present with your thoughts, you will be able to read your opponent's emotional behavior and take advantage of it.

However, if an athlete performs a specific task that is a habit, the body can and will respond up to three to five seconds before a conscious thought occurs. Take your warm-up routine, for example. If it is a routine that you have performed numerous times before, your mind may drift, and your body will just be going through the motions. You will execute the warm-up as you normally would, but the stretches and lunges may not be performed to the same extent as they would be when your mind is focused on what you are doing. Your mental and physical warm-ups are both equally important in the pre-game routine for you to play at peak condition.

To become a clutch player, staying present in your now moment is necessary for dynamic attention so you can observe the rapid changes and movements that are taking place in your line of sight.

Kansas City Chiefs quarterback Patrick Mahomes is becoming famous for his no-look pass. Tony Romo first coined the term no-look pass while commenting on the Chiefs and Ravens game on December 9, 2018.

The miraculous pass happened just before the end of the second quarter. On second and one from the Chiefs' twenty-eight-yard line, Mahomes hit wide receiver Demarcus Robinson with a short pass on the left that gained seventeen yards.

No one seeméd to notice it in the stands. But people watching on television saw it on the replay. The play started with Mahomes darting to the left, then pivoting back to the right. While evading the rush of the Ravens' defense, he quickly scanned the field for opportunities. With his head pointed directly downfield, he fired the ball diagonally across the field to his left, hitting his intended receiver.

Romo said: "Look at the magic of the quarterback, just calm, moving around dancing and then throws it. It's like almost no look."

Mahomes perfected this skill playing college ball practicing with his back-up quarterback. Even Ryan Fitzpatrick, picked up this skill at minicamp in 2018.

Many great athletes are known for their rapid responses while playing under pressure. It is a skill that may be self-taught but only if one is able to regulate one's emotions. If you can grasp the meaning of having a StillPoint presence in your mind and really know your sport, you can be a clutch player.

CHAPTER 10

Visualizations

Only he who can see the invisible can do the impossible.

-Frank L. Gaines

The practice of visualization in sports performance has been around for quite a while. Visualization practices also have had many names associated with the technique, including guided imagery, meditation, mental rehearsal, and many others. Whatever name you connect with visualization, the basic process is the same and builds upon itself with practice and set intentions.

One of the largest benefits of learning to use visuals is that it trains your mind to be in your now moment (hopefully by this point, you know what this means). Remember, it is only in the presence of your now moment that you can stay engaged with your conscious thoughts and actions that need to be performed. And just like a muscle in your body needs to be worked and trained to hold heavy objects steady, your mind needs practice and strength to hold you in the present moment for longer periods of time.

StillPoint Insight #14

In athletic physical performance, the body is nothing without the mind grounded in the present moment.

When your mind has not been coached to stay firm in the present moment for a long time, it will be too flexible and will look for anything to latch onto.

When working with visuals, you are using conscious thoughts to train your subconscious mind to think and perform how you want it to. In general terms, visualization means forming a mental image of whatever your intention is and playing it out repeatedly in your mind's eye until it becomes imprinted. It will become a memory of something you already know how to do or a goal that has already been accomplished, ready to be pulled out and repeated if needed.

A seasoned hitter doesn't consciously think about driving the outside pitch into the opposite field corner; they simply react in the moment and instinctively adjusts their swing to do so.

In your brain, you have what is known as the Reticular Activation System (RAS). Think of your RAS as the control room of your conscious thoughts. If you are focused and sitting at the helm of your conscious mind, you can give detailed messages or visuals to your brain that will deliberately set your mind to focus on any event or goal.

When I work with clients on how to perform visuals, I always give the analogy that your brain is not playing the sport for you. The brain is not running around with a little racket or golf ball in its tiny hands (assuming your brain had hands, that is). You are!

Your mind only knows that you are performing the sport because it sees you doing it. Therefore, there is no difference in seeing yourself actively playing your sport or seeing the action being played out in your mind's eye. Your RAS cannot distinguish between the physical events from the visuals you play out in your mind. Your brain will believe whatever you tell it to if there is enough emotion to support the belief of the visualization being played out in your head.

Your emotions are very important when working with visualizations. Without enough emotion, your brain will pay just enough attention to see that you are daydreaming about something unimportant. However, if you are having a heightened emotion along with your visual, it will take a direct interest in what you're doing because it feels important. Your brain will imprint it to memory for future reference.

If you are practicing affirmations or visualizations, remember that you are wasting your time if you are not feeling the impact of the achievement or performance being played out. Studies have shown that the more excitement or passion that is felt during the visuals, the more powerful and imprinted the visualization will be.

Take the time to prepare for your affirmations or visuals by invoking the feeling you are trying to accomplish before going into your practice each day. When you make any small gain toward your goal, make sure to acknowledge it with the appropriate reaction. This will help motivate your conscious mind to repeat similar experiences.

Another important aspect of visualizations that many people do not quite grasp is that to get the most out of a visual, they must incorporate their five physical senses. They need to employ sight, hearing, taste, smell, and touch to zero in on the experiences they want to perform in reality.

At first, someone may only visualize basic imagery of events along with possibly only one or two enhancements as sensory backdrops for their visuals. Think of it as daydreaming versus visualizing with intent. Daydreaming usually has no real impact on what they are trying to achieve.

When working with performance visuals, you must create the experience in your mind's eye with little to no distinctions between your reality and the simulation playing out in your mind.

Always begin your visualizations by making sure that you will not be interrupted or distracted by any outside noise or disturbance. Once you have settled in, take the time to relax and draw in a few breaths while exhaling with slightly parted lips. Hearing the breaths being exhaled will help to keep you in the present. An easy way to instantly become still in your mind is to focus on parts of your body that are moving. Wiggle your toes and ankles around, feel the inner sensation that is happening with the movement. Move your head from side to side, feel the tension releasing in your neck.

Once you are relaxed and focused, you're ready to begin your performance visual. Close your eyes and see your destination or playing field ahead of you. Make sure that you are far enough away that it will take at least fifteen to twenty steps to walk to.

StillPoint Insight #15

It is impossible to get distracted by random
thoughts if you are focused on the physical
sensations that your body is having.

As you begin walking with your destination in sight, feel your
feet connecting with the ground and sense the weight of your
body with each step. Take a moment as you are moving forward
to observe your surroundings. Is it daylight or evening? What
does the temperature feel like to you? Is your body starting to feel
the adrenaline coursing through your veins from the anticipation
of playing?

All of this primes you and prepares your mind for the
performance mental imagery that you are about to trick your
brain into believing. I always like to recommend for my clients
to use some form of a switch or trigger that signals to their mind
that the actual visualization is beginning. The switch or trigger
should be at the end of your fifteen- to twenty-step walk.

Your trigger could be a door that you will open at a gym,
or the sight and sound of a locker door being shut in a gym's
dressing room before the start of your performance. Come up
with some form of trigger that starts your visualizations, one that
can also be employed as a switch. That same trigger is equally
important when it is time for you to center your attention and put
your game face on.

By using the same trigger that is used in your visualization
and in your physical life, it will help kick-start your visualizations
much more easily in the future.

Here are a few other suggestions for you to envision when working with your performance visual imagery:

- Focus on your body's precise physical movements while in action.
- Play out the second-by-second timing of the action unfolding.
- Feel the texture and weight of anything you may encounter.
- Imagine the likely temperature of the environment as well as the bodily temperature that you would normally experience while playing.
- Feel the sweat on your brow. Imagine how your uniform feels when you sweat during play.
- Hear the sounds of your teammates or fans around you.
- Perceive the environmental sounds you normally encounter in that setting.

When using visualizations as a way of perfecting your game, try to use the memories from your previous experiences that you have already imprinted using your five physical senses. Also, zero in on the slightest details of your environment and your bodily movements. However, please remember that without feeling the emotion that you would have normally felt in real life, you might as well be daydreaming about something you would like to do.

When beginning to work with visualizations, it is easy to become distracted. Or, if you are trying to overcome a previous screw up, it is likely you may suddenly repeat the experience in your mind's eye during your visual. Please have patience with yourself. Remember, if there was a heightened emotion attached to the screw up, it was imprinted to memory and may be hard to get past initially. However, soon the bad experience will be a distant memory and will be rewritten.

Until that is accomplished, when you get distracted or hijacked by an old memory, project a big red stop sign in front of you, filling up the space in your mind's eye. And hit an imagined rewind button taking you back to the beginning of the visual, just before your trigger moment. Then let it go for the day and start fresh tomorrow.

Before long, you won't need the stop sign or rewind button when using visualizations for your performance. If you work with performance mental imagery for at least ten minutes a day, it will soon become second nature for you and add benefit to your peak performance.

Appendix

Additional Advice for Mastering your Mental Game

BREATH

- When you hold your breath, you are stopping the body's natural rhythm, the flow of oxygen in and the exhaling of nitric oxide out. Nitric oxide sends messages to your nerve cells that allows your body to react properly to outside stimuli.

- Athletes who hold their breath tend to become agitated or anxious more often during play, which leads to incoherent decision making.

- If you hold your breath while playing in a match, your muscles and organs cannot oxygenate. This may lead to dizziness and not having enough energy to finish your game or enough stamina to play at your best.

- Holding your breath before you take a swing or before throwing a ball restricts your muscles. They cannot elongate and be fluid during the swing or the throw. This is why so many great players grunt at the point of contact with the ball. When athletes grunt or make some kind of sound, it forces the air out of their lungs.

DO NOT JUDGE ANYONE, BUT MOST OF ALL DO NOT JUDGE YOURSELF

- When you judge someone or yourself negatively, it does not feel good. You generate a negative emotion as your reward every time. Even if the judgment is about someone else, a negative emotion will be attached to it, whether it is guilt or disappointment in yourself.

- When you judge a bad shot or a less-than-stellar performance for the day, you are confirming to your brain that this is how you perform, or you are telling yourself that you suck. Either one is a negative outcome. Instead, replay the correct shot in your mind or give yourself a break. Know that you will be back on your game tomorrow.

- Judgments tend to expand upon themselves. Think about it. If you were to say, *That was such a lousy serve*, it tends to lead to more lousy serves. Which in turns leads to saying to yourself *I served like **** today!* Which, of course, leads to the inevitable, *I have a terrible serve!* Stop judging yourself, give yourself a break, and know that this too shall pass if you let it go!

KISS: KEEP IT SIMPLE, STUPID

In the rare times that you do miss a shot, or if you have shanked your ball into the water, do a practice swing of the correct shot. All your brain needed was a little reminder. You got a distracted by all the chatter going on inside of your head. But after a quick perfect shadow swing, you and your brain are now both back on the same page.

BE MENTALLY AND PHYSICALLY PRESENT

Use your God-given five physical senses to help you stay present in your actions. By doing this you are giving your brain something to do so that it does not have a chance to run away from you and get caught up with the inner dialogue running around in your head. Feel the breeze touching your face. For example, feel the breath flowing in and out of your lungs. Watch your physical movements as you take your essentials out of your bag. Feel the club, ball, or racquet in your hand. These actions will help you stay in the present moment.

BE AWARE OF THE BALL

Many sports are centered around a ball. Yet not enough attention is focused on the ball. Players have such a tendency to concentrate on where they want the ball to go that they do not watch the ball meet their hands while catching it, or they do not watch the ball connect with their racquet, club, or bat.

SAY "I DON'T KNOW"

Instead of saying you know how to do something, try saying that maybe you can improve on it. I am a hard-headed athlete. Actually, I am a stubborn woman in general. So I am still learning this one myself. Be open to the fact that there is always room for improvement. Do not close your mind to the possibility that you might not know everything.

TRUST YOURSELF

- Listen to the advice of your coaches and your peers, but always listen to your own intuition when it comes to knowing what is right for you. Only you can know what the right path is for you. At the end of the day, you are the one who needs to be happy with the decisions you make.

- Trust yourself on the court or on the field. If you are in the zone and the moment calls for a shot that feels right, take it. It might not be the shot that your coaches wanted you to take, but if you feel it, do it!

- Trust your gut instincts about the big decisions in your life and trust your coaches to know how to get you there.

DO NOT BE A DRIFTER

- On average, we have over 70,000 random, mundane thoughts going through our minds every single day. And more than 90 percent of them are negative or self-deprecating. Be more aware of the activity going on upstairs.

- Set your phone to silent if you are not expecting an important call. Your social media alerts are not more important than the task that is in front of you right now, such as reading these very important tips!

- If you happen to be in the middle of a conversation with someone, make sure that you are listening to what the person sitting across from you is saying, rather than focusing on the person who is trying to get your attention by text.

- Set an intention before going into any new experience or task. What do you want to accomplish in the time allotted? What outcome do you want to achieve from the experience? By setting these intentions, you will not waste your time or energy by getting sidetracked by things that add no value to the experience.

STICKY NOTES ARE YOUR BEST FRIEND

As my clients know, I believe that sticky notes are a game- changer for efficiency. When you make a list of what you need to accomplish, your brain will not have to repeatedly remind you of them. And the bonus here is that you leave a clear pathway for insights and/or answers to come to you that will help alleviate other concerns that you may have.

In conclusion, your day will flow a lot smoother if you make notes and know what you need to accomplish rather trying to recall it from memory.

BE AWARE OF YOUR EMOTIONS

- Your emotions can either give you leverage at any given moment or they can hinder you. It is your choice. You have the control to choose one thought over another.

- Life may be fast-paced and crazy busy, so if you are not able to monitor your thoughts as you should, at least monitor your emotions. They are your foolproof way of staying on top of your game.

BONUS ADVICE

FIVE THINGS TO GIVE UP IN ORDER TO BE HAPPY

- Overthinking: Your first idea is usually the correct one.
- Fearing change: It is going to happen regardless of whether you like it or not.
- Trying to please everyone: This is impossible!
- Hanging out with negative friends: Life is too short to surround yourself with pessimistic people.
- Worrying about what others are doing: Who cares, anyway?

Glossary

Affirmations: The action or process of affirming something or being affirmed. A statement or proposition that is declared to be true.

Amygdala: The key subcortical brain center that coordinates behavioral, neural, and hormonal responses to environmental threats. It also serves as the storehouse of emotional memory within the brain. Its function is to compare incoming signals from the environment with stored emotional memories. In this way, the amygdala makes instantaneous decisions about the threat level of incoming sensory information.

Attributes: A quality or feature regarded as a characteristic or inherent part of someone or something.

Autonomic Nervous System (ANS): The portion of the nervous system that regulates most of the body's involuntary functions, including heart rate. It regulates over 90 percent of the body's functions. The heart and brain and the immune, hormonal, respiratory, and digestive systems are all connected by this network of nerves.

Awareness: Knowledge or perception of a situation or fact.

Clutch (in sport): Denoting or occurring in a critical situation in which the outcome of a game or competition is at stake.

Cognitive: Relating to cognition; concerned with the act or process of knowing, perceiving. Also, relating to the mental processes of perception, memory, judgment, and reasoning, as contrasted with emotional and volitional processes.

Coherence: Logical connectedness, internal order, or harmony among the components of a system. When a system is coherent, virtually no energy is wasted because of the internal synchronization among the parts. Increased coherence enables the emergence of new levels of creativity, cooperation, productivity, and quality physical performance.

Confidence: A feeling of self-assurance arising from one's appreciation of one's own abilities or qualities.

Consciousness: The mind's awareness of itself and the world.

Consequence: A result or effect of an action or condition of something occurring earlier.

Enhancement: An increase or improvement in quality, value, or extent.

Emotion: A strong feeling. Emotions include any of various complex reactions with both mental and physical manifestations. Examples include love, appreciation, sadness, and anger.

Emotional Intelligence: The capacity to be aware of, control, and express one's emotions, and to handle interpersonal relationships judiciously and empathetically.

Extrinsic Motivation: The reward-driven desire to accomplish something.

Flow State: Also known as being in the zone, is the mental state in which a person performing an activity is fully immersed in a feeling of energized focus, full involvement, and appreciation in the process of the activity.

Heart Rate Variability (HRV): The normally occurring beat-to-beat changes in heart rate. Analysis of HRV is an important tool used to assess the function and balance of the autonomic nervous system. HRV is considered a key indicator of aging, cardiac health, and overall well-being.

Hormonal System: The system made up of the many hormones that act and interact throughout the body to regulate many metabolic functions and the cells, organs, and tissues that manufacture them.

Hormone: A substance produced by living cells that circulates in the body's fluids and produces a specific effect on the activity of cells remote from the point of origin.

Instinct: The natural tendency of a person or animal to behave or react in a particular way.

Intrinsic Motivation: The internally driven desire to accomplish something.

Introvert: A quiet and reserved individual.

Intuition: Intelligence and understanding that bypasses the logical, linear cognitive processes; the faculty of direct knowing, as if by instinct, without conscious reasoning.

Judgments: Strongly held, largely negative attitudes and opinions often based on incomplete and prejudicial information.

Morse Code: An alphabet or code in which letters are represented by combinations of long and short signals of light or sound.

Neurotransmitter: The body's chemical messengers. They are the molecules used by the nervous system to transmit messages between neurons, or from neurons to muscles.

Parasympathetic: The branch of the autonomic nervous system that slows or relaxes bodily functions. This part of the nervous system is analogous to the brakes in a car.

Perception: The act or faculty of apprehending by means of the senses; the way an individual views a situation or event. How we perceive an event or an issue underlies how we think, feel, and react to that event or issue.

Perspective: A particular attitude toward or way of regarding something; point of view.

Post-Traumatic Stress Disorder (PTSD): A psychiatric disorder that can occur in people who have experienced or witnessed a traumatic event such as a natural disaster, a serious car accident, a terrorist act, war/combat, rape, or other violent personal assault.

Proactive: Creating or controlling a situation by causing something to happen rather than responding to it after it has happened.

Reactive: Acting in response to a situation rather than creating or controlling it.

Resilience: The capacity to recover quickly from difficulties; toughness.

Resistance: The refusal to accept or comply with something; the attempt to prevent something by action or argument. To push against.

Reticular Activation System (RAS): A diffuse network of nerve pathways in the brainstem connecting the spinal cord, cerebrum, and cerebellum, and mediating the overall level of consciousness.

Self-Regulation: Controlling one's behavior, emotions, and thoughts in the pursuit of short and long-term goals; the ability to manage disruptive emotions and impulses.

Situational Awareness: The perception of environmental elements.

Stress: Pressure, strain, or a sense of inner turmoil resulting from our perceptions and reactions to events or conditions. A state of negative emotional arousal, usually associated with feelings of discomfort or anxiety that we attribute to our circumstances or situation.

Subconscious: Concerning the part of the mind of which one is not fully aware but which influences one's actions and feelings.

Sympathetic: The branch of the autonomic nervous system that speeds up bodily functions, preparing us for mobilization and action. The fight-or-flight response to stress activates the sympathetic nervous system and causes the contraction of blood vessels along with a rise in the heart rate and many other bodily responses. This part of the nervous system is analogous to the gas pedal in a car.

Visualizations: Any technique for creating images, diagrams, or animations to communicate a message to oneself or to someone else; the formation of a mental image of something.

Printed in the United States
by Baker & Taylor Publisher Services